Creation,
Power,
and
Truth

Creation, Power, and Truth

The Gospel in a World
of Cultural Confusion

N. T. Wright

ZONDERVAN

Creation, Power, and Truth
Copyright © 2013 by The Society for Promoting Christian Knowledge. Text by Tom Wright.

Published in Grand Rapids, Michigan, by Zondervan. Zondervan is a registered trademark of The Zondervan Corporation, L.L.C., a wholly owned subsidiary of HarperCollins Christian Publishing, Inc.

Requests for information should be addressed to customercare@harpercollins.com.

Original edition published in English under the title *Creation, Power and Truth: The Gospel In A World Of Cultural Confusion* by:

SPCK
Publishing part of SPCK Group
London, England, UK
www.spck.org.uk

ISBN 978-0-310-17292-5 (softcover)
ISBN 978-0-310-17294-9 (audio)
ISBN 978-0-310-17293-2 (ebook)

Cover design: Micah Kandros Design
Cover image: Shutterstock

Printed in the United States of America
25 26 27 28 29 LBC 5 4 3 2 1

To a Wise and Generous Friend

Contents

Preface

This book is based on the Noble Lectures which I was privileged to give in the Memorial Chapel at Harvard University in the autumn of 2006, as the guest of the Revd Professor Peter Gomes. I was and am very grateful to Peter for the invitation and for his cheerful and engaging hospitality. I have not attempted to add very much to what was said in the lectures, except for some tidying up and light editing, in view of the official 'responses' I received at the time from Professors François Bovon, Sarah Coakley and David Hempton. I am very grateful to them all. Harvard has been a special place for me ever since I was a visiting professor there myself in 1999, and it was a delight to renew old friendships and to be able to test out ideas with a friendly but not uncritical audience.

As will become apparent, the book is an attempt to bridge a gulf. People who write about current cultural and political matters, even from a Christian point of view, do not often engage with the Bible in any detail. Biblical scholars regularly repay the compliment. We are all inevitably specialists these days, and we know the dangers of intruding in subject areas where we are less qualified. Nevertheless, the attempt must be made from time to time, and it seemed to me that since I was living at the time with one foot in the world of biblical scholarship and the other in the world of current affairs in both church and state there was something to be said for having a go. When I thought my way through the various issues that seemed to me important and realized that the material would fall nicely into a Trinitarian pattern I decided that the three-lecture invitation from Harvard had found its answer.

Things have moved on, of course. The original lectures were given when the Iraq conflict was in full swing. Dan Brown's book *The Da Vinci Code* was still being widely discussed. But the issues raised thereby have not gone away. If anything, they have intensified in complexity. The topics are still not only relevant but in my view urgent. As this book was going to press, I came upon a new novel by the bestselling Brazilian author Paulo Coelho, entitled *Manuscript Found in Accra* (New York: Alfred A. Knopf, 2013). It purports to be a transcription of the wise teachings of a 'Copt', given in 1099 when the Crusaders were about to invade Jerusalem. In fact it contains numerous 'wisdom' sayings, some of which echo Kahlil Gibran, some of which sound a bit like the teaching of Jesus, and most of which sound like classic, dreamy postmodern quasi-spirituality. Coelho writes a preface in which he hints at a tenuous link between this 'document' and the so-called gnostic 'gospels' found at Nag Hammadi. There follows a passage which is pure Dan Brown, suggesting that the four gospels in the New Testament were selected from a much larger set of possible contenders for reasons that many today would regard as spurious. Once again, what we are offered, by implication over and against the teaching of the four canonical gospels, is a soft, squashy version of Gnosticism: 'Who we are, what we fear, and what we hope for the future come from the knowledge and belief that can be found within us, and not from the adversity that surrounds us' (quoted from the book's dust jacket). The immense popularity of this kind of thing shows that the appeal of Gnosticism is as powerful today as when I gave the original lectures.

The Noble lectures were founded by Nannie Yulee Noble. Her stated aim was 'to arouse in young people, and primarily in the students of that great university, the joy of service for Christ and humanity, especially in the ministry of the Christian Church'. I hope I have in some measure contributed to that cause.

Tom Wright

Preface to the North American edition

This book is based on the Noble Lectures that I gave at Harvard some years ago. In it, I am deliberately striking some notes that all too often get forgotten: the doctrine of God's good creation and his intention to remake it. Because these themes have often been overlooked—for instance, when many Christians focus either simply on "making this world a better place" or on "how to leave this world and go to heaven instead"—whole swathes of biblical and theological truth have been ignored, and we are all the poorer for that.

In particular, the Christian doctrine of creation itself—the idea that the one God made a good world and intends to remake it—undermines the fashionable "gnosticism" of much Western culture. "Gnosticism" was all about "discovering who I really am" by introspection in the search for this or that "identity," which easily leads into forms of narcissism—helped on its way in today's electronic culture. To rediscover what the Bible says about creation is to sense the fresh air of new possibilities that can lead us out of that trap.

"Power" has often been a dirty word in our culture, as many have recognized that politicians and rulers have exercised their power in bullying, cheating, and dehumanizing those at their mercy. But the New Testament offers a vision of true power, which remains paradoxical (St. Paul says that power is made perfect in weakness) but which, when we see its roots in the story of Jesus, emerges as the power, not of self-seeking but of self-giving love.

Likewise, the idea of truth has been at a discount in our culture. We all know about "fake news," conspiracy theories, and the way some people talk of "my truth" and "your truth" as though all truth-claims were simply about "the way we see things" rather than about the real world. But it is that real world—as loved by the God of creation whose power is now focused on bringing healing and new creation—that offers the grounding for fresh statements of truth, truth that (like true power) will challenge self-seeking distortions.

When we look at these three, creation, power, and truth, we discover that they have a Trinitarian shape. God the Father is the Creator; God the Son is the one to whom, for the early Christians, all power has been given, though it remains a power shaped by his crucifixion; the Holy Spirit is the Spirit of truth, the agent of the new creation that provides the bedrock for new and life-giving truth claims.

This little book, then, offers a series of entry points into some of the key questions of our day. I am inviting readers to consider the crucial ways in which the Christian gospel itself challenges and subverts the intellectual, moral, and political values that pervade our contemporary culture. I hope that people reading this short book will be stimulated not only to fresh thought and prayer but to wise decision-making regarding common cultural assumptions and controlling narratives, past and present. We need to grow a new generation of thoughtful, biblically oriented Christians who know how hear, speak, and live the gospel of Christ in a world of cultural confusion. And I hope this book will help them do that.

N. T. Wright
Wycliffe Hall, Oxford

Introduction

The subject of this book is the challenge of today's and tomorrow's culture, and the resources in the Christian gospel, and the scriptures Christians read, with which to address those challenges. We are under enormous pressure in these days as the tectonic plates of Western culture slide this way and that, throwing up moral, social and political earthquakes and tsunamis to right and left. I want to reflect on three cultural pressures and the way they interact, and I suggest that this reflection will help us to see where we are in the confusing and disturbing times we face in our church and in the wider world.

I begin with a fascinating reflection borrowed from an article in *The Times* (4 February 2006) by the Chief Rabbi, Sir Jonathan Sacks (now Lord Sacks). Dr Sacks is one of the most highly and widely respected commentators on the contemporary scene in Britain. He writes about the wanderings of the children of Israel through the wilderness, and suggests two images for our own pilgrim pathway.

The first is the new electronic toy, the global positioning, or satellite-navigation, system, which sits in your car and tells you where to turn in order to get where you need to go. He points out that for many men in particular – particularly, he says, Jewish men, on which I couldn't possibly comment – this is counter-intuitive: fancy having someone else's voice, quite possibly a woman's voice, telling you where to turn the car! So, he says, we behave like the Israelites in the wilderness, who had God in their midst to guide them: we hear the voice, but deliberately turn somewhere else, in the wrong direction. There is then a pause, after which the voice says, in effect: Well, this wasn't what we had in mind; but since we're now here, you will now need to turn round, to do this, and that, in order to get back on track. Thank God, says Dr Sacks, that even when we take a wrong turning, perhaps deliberately, he will go along with us and pick us up from where we've landed ourselves and get us back on track in the end.

But not always, and not necessarily. In contrast to the image of the in-car navigation system, Dr Sacks points out that there is another kind of wandering which doesn't carry the same guarantee of ultimate rescue. There is a certain kind of ant, he says – again, I wouldn't be able to comment on this but I take his word for it – which, when it's lost, is programmed to follow the ant in front. This normally works fine, because ants are pretty smart and someone up ahead will surely know where we're all going. But sometimes, apparently, the ones up ahead will start to circle round, looking for another ant to follow . . . and another, and another . . . and before too long all the ants will be going round and round, convinced they are marching in the right direction but all merely following one another in a great circle. And the result is catastrophic. They will all die.

The question we face today, inside the church but just as much outside it in our wider Western culture, is whether despite all our blunderings we are still in fact listening for a voice from elsewhere, a guiding voice which will get us out of the mess and back on track to human and Christian flourishing, or whether we are in fact merely following one another round and round in a circle, convinced we're doing the right thing but heading for futility and starvation. Will the church, and the world, do the satellite-navigation thing or the ant thing?

In order to come at this question I want to plot three elements of our contemporary culture and to point out the ways in which they interact with each other, and the ways in particular in which they condition the debates and puzzles we face in the church and the wider world. Unless we reflect on these very different challenges, and the way they shape our society and the lives of the millions of individuals who make it up, we shall be walking around blindfold, shutting our eyes to the hidden but persuasive forces which put pressure on those among whom we live and work, and indeed on ourselves too. I choose these three; there are no doubt many others. And I shall then argue, on the basis of the New Testament, that to follow the living Jesus gives us the resources both to face these challenges for ourselves and to enable the work of the gospel and of God's kingdom to go ahead, to get back on track, to find the way to health and life. The three challenges are the contemporary versions of Gnosticism and imperialism, and then the apparently new (but in fact very old) phenomenon known as postmodernism.

1

God the creator in a world of neo-Gnosticism

My aim in this book is to raise three key questions about our contemporary culture: to make connections, to suggest an interplay of assumptions and controlling narratives within today's world, and so to offer a rough sketch-map of certain aspects of contemporary culture on which we may discern key trends and link together some powerful ideas. At the same time I shall look afresh at certain aspects of the biblical story and draw out some often unnoticed themes.

I have used a traditional Trinitarian framework. But I approach this 'from below', coming at it through the exegesis of particular biblical passages and themes, rather than imposing it heavy-handedly as a dogmatic stereotype. I aim to re-read familiar biblical material with contemporary concerns in mind. I have increasingly found resonances between ancient and contemporary culture; exploring these is risky, but it remains full of potential.

Glimpses of *gnosis* in Western modernity

We live, I suggest, in a world characterized by certain types of Gnosticism. One of the most glaring recent signs of this is the extraordinary popularity of Dan Brown's *The Da Vinci Code*.[1] This book was a runaway bestseller when it was first published in 2004, and it has had an enormous impact on the imagination of a whole generation. In that novel, Brown taps into a deep desire in our culture for *hidden knowledge*, a secret understanding whose possessor can pierce the mystery, find the key to life, and in particular discover the buried truth about his or her own true identity. In his many books, but particularly in this one, Dan Brown has been saying things people in our day want to hear so badly that they are prepared to swallow ridiculous and unhistorical proposals in large quantity as long as they get the worldview they want.

In form, the book is a seemingly endless sequence of conspiracy theories, of the penetration of one secret after another. In substance, the plot hinges on the great conspiracy theory widely believed today: that Christianity as we have known it (not least Roman Catholicism) is based on a gigantic mistake, a huge cover-up, perpetrated by the second and subsequent Christian generations, including the writers of the canonical gospels, hiding the early and true person and message of Jesus himself behind self-serving ecclesial propaganda. Like many other writers in recent times, Dan Brown has offered us a mixture of seriously proposed scholarly theories and historically ridiculous notions, especially that of Jesus having a child by Mary Magdalene and starting a royal blood line whose current carrier is the unwitting heroine of the novel, who thereby finally discovers 'who she really is'. The average reader, innocent of genuine ancient history, is left with the impression that the church has hushed up the 'real Jesus', not least Jesus' own programme for discovering the 'sacred feminine'.

The phenomenal success of this book is the index of a cultural trend: the pursuit of hidden knowledge whose bearer will have the privileged inside track on the meaning of life, backed up by esoteric traditions purporting to be about Jesus. At this level we notice obvious parallels with ancient Gnosticism.

One word about the problem of description. We have recently been cautioned against assuming that there was any one 'thing' called 'Gnosticism'.[2] The evidence is pluriform and often confusing; generalizations can mislead; we should perhaps talk of 'Gnosticisms', plural, just as some have spoken of ancient 'Judaisms' and 'Christianities'. And yet, for the plural itself to have any meaning, there must be a corresponding singular, however generalized.[3] Certainly, along with those who see multiple varieties of Gnosticism in the ancient world, plenty of equally erudite scholars are still content to speak of several broad defining features – culled from gnostic writings themselves, not simply from their opponents.[4]

Debates abound as to how many key elements it takes before we say 'Gnosticism'. But the major elements are well known and scarcely controversial – especially since they cohere closely. I highlight four. First, cosmological dualism: the world of space, time and matter is secondary and/or shabby, dangerous and/or downright wicked. Second, this world was made by a secondary deity, at best incompetent and at worst malevolent. Third, the solution is to escape, to some kind of Platonic heaven. Fourth, the escape route is *gnosis*, knowledge, of the crucial secrets – about the world, about the true god and the bad creator god, and, centrally and vitally, about oneself. *Discovering who you really are* lies at the heart of it: more particularly, discovering that deep down you are one of the sparks of light, imprisoned within the present material world but longing to escape. This quadruple ancient worldview took many forms, including some with Jewish features, some with Christian, and some with both. But this fourfold scheme is well enough known and, with significant variations, widespread in the ancient world.

We note other regular emphases: the elitism of those who attain this *gnosis*; the necessary rejection of bodily resurrection and of a final judgment through which the present world will be put to rights; and conspiracy theories about the parent religions (reading the Hebrew scriptures upside down, with Cain as a hero and YHWH as a villain; subverting the Christian gospels with secret teachings of Jesus). There is of course much more to ancient Gnosticism than this, but these features appear frequently.

Early Christian opponents of Gnosticism highlighted the ancient Jewish doctrine of creation. That, indeed, was a major reason why the early Christians appropriated and reinterpreted the Hebrew scriptures. They weren't simply snatching texts away from Jewish interlocutors, but were determinedly understanding Jesus and Christian faith in terms of the creational monotheism of Genesis, the psalms and the prophets. What mattered to them, as of foundational importance, was God's kingdom coming on earth as in heaven, with all the political and social implications that flowed from that. For this, they needed a strong doctrine of creation.

With all this in the background, I want to suggest, in line with other contemporary writers, that we should understand some key elements of today's culture in terms of modern types of Gnosticism.[5] Dan Brown is only the tip of the iceberg. Let me briefly sketch the relevant features. (This isn't, by the way, a matter of picking up a complete package from the second or third century and observing it repeated in our own day. For a start, as we noted, there is no single, coherent pattern of ancient Gnosticism. For another, the relevant features are themselves various, not entirely coherent, with different degrees of correspondence to their ancient counterparts. Nevertheless, with these caveats I believe that we can and should identify, and critique, an overall gnostic mood in our own day.)

To begin with, so obvious that it might be missed, there is the modern self-description: the Enlightenment. We are the enlightened ones, who have emerged from the murky world of superstition like Plato's cave-dwellers coming out into the light. Our science and technology set us apart; our politics are superior by definition; our artistic and cultural achievements are 'the classics'. Our maps place Western Europe in the golden section; our grand narratives of world history lead up to the eschatological moment when humankind 'came of age', leaving behind our ancient and medieval infancy. We are the elite, carrying in nineteenth-century Europe 'the white man's burden' to bring enlightenment to the world, and in twentieth- and twenty-first-century America the 'manifest destiny' to rule the world as God's chosen people. We have discovered who we are, and are thereby set apart, glimpsing different possibilities from ordinary mortals, and moreover being subject to different rules.

Enlightenment ontology grounds our elitism in a radical dualism. Lessing's ugly ditch between the necessary truths of reason and the contingent truths of history has been broadened into almost all areas of life, resulting in a world where most westerners automatically assume that faith and public life must be held carefully apart. Whole societies, notably that of the United States of America, have been founded on this assumption, which then generates all kinds of debates, from the propriety of school prayers to slogans printed on banknotes. And this dualism has a great deal in common with that of ancient Gnosticism.

Such dualism has expressed itself in two quite different ways, corresponding broadly to the division between asceticism and libertinism with which its critics charged ancient Gnosticism. The ancient Gnostics sometimes regarded the body as trash to be shunned, and sometimes as an irrelevant object which could therefore be used to do whatever one felt like, without consequences on other levels.

Thus we have seen, on the one hand, the 'ascetic' route: don't let your spirituality get entangled with the real world of space, time and (particularly) matter. Nineteenth-century Western Christianity made a virtue of its otherworldly present spirituality and future hope. It is not surprising that the word 'resurrection', which sixteenth- and seventeenth-century Christians well knew referred to an embodied future life, has been flattened into a fancy way of talking about 'going to heaven when you die.'[6] The author of the *Treatise on the Resurrection* (a gnostic tract most likely from the late second century) would have approved. On a wider level, much religious devotion has regularly kept itself well clear of politics and public life. Part of the shock in the USA of the rise of the 'religious right' – and part of the shock in the UK of an increasingly vocal 'Christian left' – has been the category mistake, as opponents see it, of mixing up what 'everybody knows' ought to be kept apart. This is the ascetic route.

Equally, many have gone the 'libertine' route: the world is irrelevant to God and to our spiritual agendas, so we can do what we like with it. Within the heaven/earth dualism, those who want to carve up the world with machines, social systems and empires may do so without hindrance. If there is a god, this being is distant, and doesn't care what we do in or to this stupid old world. This functional atheism, in which society remains immune to a critique which, in any case, the escapist churches had no intention of offering, led increasingly to actual atheism. When A. N. Wilson wrote his book *God's Funeral,*[7] he was talking about the nineteenth century, not the 'death-of-god' movement of the 1960s.

Thus Western society, in contrast to many other societies including those of Native North Americans, has seen itself as having carte blanche to treat the created order as if it were our private gold mine – or oil well! – on the one hand and our private rubbish dump on the other. At the individual level, the great controlling myth of our time has been the belief that within each of us there is a real, inner, private 'self', long buried beneath layers of socialization and attempted cultural and religious control, and needing to be rediscovered if we are to live authentic lives. When we 'discover' this 'true inner self', we must do whatever it dictates, even if it means ignoring the norms of the 'unenlightened' society all around us. Perhaps half the novels written today, perhaps two-thirds of the Hollywood movies, have this as their subtext. More worryingly, perhaps three-quarters of contemporary Western religion has gone along for the ride. In terms of the image I quoted from Jonathan Sacks in the Introduction to this book, I regard this trend as bearing the marks of a society copying the ants rather than the satellite-navigation system.

At the centre of this theme we find that classic gnostic move, the appeal to 'experience' over against other authorities, resulting in the relentless quest to 'find out who I really am'. The word 'experience' is of course very slippery, with echoes on the one hand of the Reformers' appeal to a living and vital religion over against a dead formalism, and on the other hand of the Wesleyan insistence on an actual *experience* of sanctification as a fresh gift from God. But in our day this same word, with its quite proper overtones of real personal faith as against sterile outward conformism, is placed within a quite different narrative, that of the Gnosticism which declares that the outer world, both the wider world of society and the church and the outward world of my physical body, are irrelevant and indeed misleading, and that I must find within myself the spark of life and truth by which to reorder my whole existence.

But there is no room for complacency on the orthodox front. Those of us who argue for classic Christian belief and morality in today's church must come to terms with the fact that we, too, have all too often colluded with the gnostic imperative. It is sadly possible to tick all the 'correct' doctrinal and ethical boxes, to learn to pronounce all the shibboleths, but to put them all within the wrong controlling narrative – like a child who manages to join up all the dots in a follow-the-dots picture but produces a donkey instead of an elephant. Precisely because, in the world of the Enlightenment, abstract doctrines and rules have often predominated over narratives (despite the fact that the Bible itself would suggest that it should be the other way round), the church has often simply not noticed that you can affirm the Trinity, the incarnation, the atonement, the resurrection, the call to bodily holiness, and still work within a narrative which colludes with Gnosticism. That is precisely what happens when orthodox Christians think, speak, pray and live as though the main aim of the game were simply to 'go to heaven when you die', embracing a private, detached spirituality in the present and a world-denying and escapist eschatology in the future. We can criticize the second-century Gnostics for their redefinition of the word 'resurrection' so as to mean, not a new bodily life after a time of being bodily dead, but a spiritual life in the present and hereafter; but this position is, worryingly, held just as much by those post-Enlightenment pietists and evangelicals whose major and overriding concern was to stress 'heaven' as the Christian's true home, and who used the word 'resurrection' as a metaphor for going to that home at last. It is thus possible to hold the essentially gnostic narrative while also affirming the great Christian doctrines, without noticing that all of them, not least the incarnation and the resurrection, actually tell heavily against it. And we can do so without noticing in particular how this deconstructs the prayer Jesus taught us to pray, which no gnostic could ever pray, that God's kingdom will come on earth as in heaven. The enormous resistance to this line of thought, and the insistence on escaping from the messy world of politics and culture in favour of a 'spiritual' gospel, shows, I'm afraid, that a great deal of orthodoxy, not least the orthodox evangelicalism which I know rather well from the inside, has to look in the mirror and admit that it has colluded with Gnosticism. And this very same Gnosticism, paradoxically, also drives the cultural and theological agendas which orthodoxy quite rightly, in my view, is currently opposing. Significantly, too, this is the kind of orthodoxy which insists that it alone knows the way to heaven, so that you have to believe what you're told and do what you're told to go there; the classic powerful system, in other words, against which so many on the left in today's churches have explicitly and angrily reacted. Unless we are prepared to get inside this whole model and rethink not only our orthodox doctrines but the orthodox narrative within which they make sense, our debates will collapse into dialogues of the deaf, and we shall be deaf, too, to the divine navigation system which would lead us out of the mess. God save us from the circular ant-trap of Gnosticism, ancient or modern.

The results, after all, are obvious. They have been chronicled by various commentators over the last two or three decades. In particular, Tom Wolfe pointed out a generation ago in his novel *The Bonfire of the Vanities* that this kind of Gnosticism leads directly to the confusion, which has grown apace since he wrote, over sexual identity and behaviour[8]. If the outside world, including my own body in its male or female particularity, are not the good creation of a good and wise God, but rather the inessentials made by a blind and stupid creator, and if instead my inner 'experience' is what really counts, then I not only can but must be true to the spark of light, and indeed of desire, which I find most deeply within myself, even if it goes contrary to the apparent order of creation, the norms of traditional society, and the teaching of the Bible and the church. What is more, in doing so I do not need to claim some space for myself out on the left margin of morality. On the contrary, I am a religious hero for acting as I have. The power of that rhetoric today, in church and world alike, shows that Gnosticism is alive and well. And unless we see it for what it is, and learn how not only to answer it but to answer truly the deep longings which drive people towards it, we shall be ministering the gospel, and debating the key issues that face us in the church, with one hand tied behind our backs. It isn't simply a question of whether this or that behaviour is right or wrong. It's a question of the large, implicit controlling narratives to which our culture, and our church, has become enthralled.

Notice, indeed, how this works out within the church. Many in our churches declare themselves scandalized by the kind of argument I have just described; but look under the surface and you may find the same thing in a different guise. If you regard the present space-time universe as a dark, bad place, the abode of evil forces, what you will need is an escape mechanism. That is precisely what is offered by the highly popular 'Left Behind' theology, which forms the most obvious right-wing variety of contemporary Gnosticism. The elect will be snatched away to glory, leaving the world to stew in its own juices. This then justifies ecological carelessness on the one hand and military conquest on the other, not least in the Middle East, since the promised Armageddon needs to happen anyway and the sooner the better.

But when churches get involved in all this – as they most surely do – it makes sense to ask: which 'god' might we be talking about, anyway? This double-edged dualism, the ascetics on the one hand and the libertines on the other, highlights a controversy which has become increasingly ironic as it has rumbled on. Do we or don't we believe in a good god who made the world? This was a key element in much ancient Gnosticism, for whose adherents the creator of the universe was muddled or even malevolent. The pains and sorrows of life within the present world could therefore be explained not as the intrusion of evil into a good creation but as the result of bad planning, workmanship and management. Today's leading Darwinian, Richard Dawkins, regards the Old Testament's creator God in pretty much the same way. YHWH, he declares, is

> arguably the most unpleasant character in all fiction: jealous and proud of it; a petty, unjust, unforgiving control-freak; a vindictive, bloodthirsty ethnic cleanser; a misogynistic, homophobic, racist, infanticidal, genocidal, filicidal, pestilential, megalomaniacal, sadomasochistic, capriciously malevolent bully.

He is, suggests Dawkins, the 'most unlovely instantiation' of the 'God hypothesis', along with his 'insipidly opposite Christian face', that of 'Gentle Jesus meek and mild'.[9] Dawkins refers, as he often does, to Thomas Jefferson, who stated that 'the Christian God is a being of terrific character – cruel, vindictive, capricious and unjust'. This denunciation of the ancient Hebrew God belongs with second-century thinkers such as Marcion and Valentinus. But life then gets more complicated, since Darwinians don't think that this god actually made the world. They have produced a new version of the old dualism: creation and its natural processes are good, and the god who *pretended* to have made them is bad – thus projecting on to the hypothetical creator the bloodletting and selfishness of natural selection. Tellingly, Dawkins speaks of himself and other evolutionary biologists as those who have had their 'consciousness raised' so that they can see things others can't. Even some of his fellow-scientists, not least some of the leading physicists, have apparently not realized that natural selection will explain more or less everything: they have not had their consciousnesses raised. This is the classic language of Gnosticism. Dawkins even proposes a new name for those who have learned the secrets of the world: they are the 'Brights'. They are the elite, understanding the mysteries of the universe. Even their as yet unsubstantiated hypotheses about life itself are, a priori, superior to all others.

But here is the further irony. Those who objected to Darwin in the first place, and those who still fight against his theories in the name of 'creationism' or 'intelligent design', regularly show that they, too, live within the split-level world of contemporary Gnosticism. It is no accident that our continuing debates about creation and evolution have rumbled on alongside the gnostic tendencies in our culture. But the problem has then been that, just as some (certainly not all) evolutionists have had their eyes firmly on the deconstruction of the Christian doctrine of creation, so some (certainly not all) of the creationists have thought simply of validating the Bible for its own sake, while continuing paradoxically to hold some form of Gnosticism at the level of the larger narrative. The anti-evolution agenda (to generalize for a moment) is driven by those who claim, and seek to prove, that the Bible is literally true. But when they have proved a six-day creation, they do not leave us with the fully biblical theology in which the creator God will redeem the world, renewing it so as to make new heavens and new earth, but essentially with the same dualist, even gnostic, theology: an otherworldly spirituality in the present, an otherworldly hope in the future, and a vacuum where there should be serious political critique.[10] So-called 'creationism' is, in my experience, wrongly labelled, because it does not take seriously, as the second- and third-century Christian teachers did, the full meaning of the assertion that the God we know *in and through Jesus Christ* remains committed to his creation and will one day put it to rights, renewing it from top to bottom. My point is this: that the debates about creation which have characterized Western culture have largely taken place *within* an essentially gnostic framework, an assumed dualism which has itself largely gone unchallenged.

Note, too, the paradox that then arises. There are would-be religious 'conservatives' in today's Western culture who oppose Darwinism on the grounds that it is anti-biblical. But that same society, often with the enthusiastic support of the same people, regularly insists upon a large-scale *social* Darwinism in which the doctrine of the 'survival of the fittest' is applied relentlessly to the global rights of the superpower. To do this means either that you rescue an apparent allegiance to one part of the Bible while ruthlessly denying and suppressing the larger biblical narrative and imperative, or that you invoke the blind forces of social evolution, which, like the forces that produced the dinosaurs, can just as easily remove those at present in power. Back to the large circle of dead ants.

The cosmological dualism which has permeated all these debates has generated a religious mood which some writers have seen as the default mode for Western culture, with the USA leading the way and Western Europe eager to follow: the cult of self-discovery. Finding out 'who I really am', delving deep to discern hidden identity underneath social conditioning and traditional belief, is assumed to be central to the religious quest, corresponding to the ancient gnostic notion of salvation not by a gift of grace from outside oneself but by the revelation of buried truth within. Here we note the cultural imperative towards psychology and its offshoots. As Carl Jung famously said, 'Who looks outside, dreams; who looks inside, awakens'. The result, exactly in line with ancient Gnosticism, is that the real locus of authority is neither in the creator God, nor in the world that he made, nor in the Bible, nor even in Jesus, but in oneself and one's own 'experience'.

This became almost comically clear in the early comments on the translation and publication of the ancient gnostic tract which has been named *The Gospel of Judas*. The editors of the newly discovered text made it clear that for them this wasn't just an interesting historical document, but rather a vital clue to a more exciting form of Christianity than dull, boring old orthodoxy. The canonical Jesus instructed his followers to deny themselves and take up their cross. The gnostic Jesus tells you to discover yourself and follow your own star.[11] Considering how obscure, and actually how depressing, many of the ancient gnostic texts are, it is remarkable how readily people today grasp at them in the conviction that they offer a viable and indeed vibrant way forward over against what are assumed to be the stultifying and sterile pathways of mainstream Christian faith.

All this is held in place, within the contemporary church and world, by a massive conspiracy theory which I have else-where described as a new 'myth of Christian origins'. This widespread narrative, enthusiastically propagated by many books, magazine articles, television programmes, and (not least) sermons and apparently 'Christian' teaching, serves to support the prevailing worldview. In this myth, Jesus was just a good man who did not see himself as the son of God, nor his death as redemptive; he did not rise from the dead. Instead of announcing the inbreaking into this world of the kingdom of the creator God, he taught a new type of gnostic or spiritual wisdom, a path of spiritual self-discovery or even self-improvement. The canonical gospels were written much later, and were then canonized as a deliberate move to squelch that early and exciting spirituality and to offer instead a formalized and institutionalized religion, on its way to conformity with the Roman empire. They, along with the rest of developing 'orthodoxy', were anticipating the Constantinian settlement and trying to become more socially and culturally respectable. They thus modified and falsified the original message of Jesus. We must therefore, according to this new myth, get back in touch with the original message of Jesus, in order to reconnect with a wisdom or *gnosis* less like traditional Christianity and more like other, wider movements of spirituality.

This leaves you with what the ancient Gnostics were offering: a religion of self-discovery in which one acquires the 'knowledge', or *gnosis*, that one is already a spark of light, and can thereby escape from the wicked world of space, time and matter, and enjoy a private and detached spirituality in the present and an escapist heaven hereafter, relating not to the wicked creator God, the God of Israel, but to some quite different and higher deity. This is an enormously attractive prospect, not least for many who were brought up within traditional Catholic or Protestant homes, and who see themselves as having escaped from hard-edged and constricting forms of Christianity precisely by embracing some kind of neo-Gnosticism.

Such people were the primary market for a book like Dan Brown's, which not only expounded the new myth of Christian origins and the large-scale conspiracy theory which it presupposes, but did so with a plot which was itself a labyrinthine series of interlocking conspiracy theories. At the level of both content and structure, therefore, the book has been enormously attractive to many in our society, for nameable and quantifiable reasons. Many who feel alienated either from the church of their youth or from the wider society of power and money are eager to believe that it's all a plot, that there is after all a better way for them to live, and that the rich and powerful have hushed it all up in order to stop us having a good time, to prevent us getting in touch with what 'Jesus' really taught. No amount of pointing out that what Brown writes is historical nonsense has prevented people wanting his underlying message to be true, both in its structure and in its content. Many of those people are in our churches today. The worldview into which they have slid, often without realizing it, shapes their perception of what being Christian is all about.

In fact, as various writers have shown, Gnosticism is the default mode for modern Western religion in general. I think of such different works as Philip Lee's remarkable book, *Against the Protestant Gnostics*, Harold Bloom's *The American Religion* and Cyril O'Regan's *Gnostic Return in Modernity*. For all that such writers sometimes exaggerate, and leave themselves open to challenge at various points, the overall case remains very strong. The Enlightenment assured us that we Westerners were indeed the 'enlightened' ones, set apart from the rest of humanity. And the religion sanctioned by the Enlightenment was precisely a variety of Gnosticism: leave behind the messy world of the public square, of politics and business and government, and escape into your private relationship with God now and in the ultimate future. The prevailing secularism, in fact, produces Gnosticism as its co-operative bedfellow: secularists can run the world while the religious cultivate their private spirituality. Both will then react angrily against any attempt to get religion back into public life, and will sometimes label such attempts as 'fundamentalist' – which isn't surprising, because there is such a thing as fundamentalism and it's on the rise. So the split between the real world and the spiritual aspiration continues. The new 'myth of Christian origins' is designed to escape the former and embrace the latter.

This isn't the place to argue historically against this new myth. I have done that elsewhere.[12] Sufficient to note two things in particular.

First, on persecution and social acceptability. The second-century Christians who were being thrown to the lions and burnt at the stake were not reading *The Gospel of Thomas* or *The Gospel of Judas* or other similar documents. They were reading Matthew, Mark, Luke and John, and were finding in those books, not a socially acceptable or culturally conformist faith, but one which declared that Jesus was Lord and that Caesar wasn't – the faith we shall examine in more detail in Chapter 2. The Gnostics were sometimes persecuted, but by and large they escaped: escapism was, after all, what they were about. Even if some did see themselves as Christians, the Romans were not likely to regard them as subversive. They were not, in fact, interested in God's kingdom coming on earth as in heaven, but rather in a non-confrontational heavenly kingdom. And in the last two centuries of our own era this new myth of Christian origins has grown up precisely where the church has colluded deeply and explicitly with the secular Enlightenment in accepting the great gulf between faith and real life.[13]

Second, on resurrection: part of the rhetoric of the Enlightenment has been to claim for itself the discovery that dead people do not rise. I have often heard this trumpeted as a new thing, whereas of course everyone from Homer to Virgil, from Plato to Pliny, knew that dead people stayed dead. We didn't need Copernicus, Newton, Rousseau or Voltaire to tell us that. Belief in Jesus' resurrection always was, in the early church, not a matter of people believing in odd miracles because they didn't know the laws of nature, but rather of believing that the creator God had acted afresh within his world to launch his new creation in and through Jesus himself. The rejection of Jesus' resurrection (and, usually, of the final resurrection of all God's people) within post-Enlightenment theology is therefore not, as it often makes itself out to be, the result of new knowledge or fresh insight. It is, rather, a structural necessity within a world where belief in God as creator, and in God as final judge – the twin beliefs which together entail resurrection – have been rejected in favour of some kind of Gnosticism. It is high time to turn the modernist critique on itself, and to enquire what interests, social and cultural, have been served by the frantic insistence both that Jesus cannot have been raised and that we know this today with a new kind of certainty.

As with creationism, however, so with the resurrection: at this point there emerges the irony of a fundamentalist Christianity that affirms bodily resurrection but for the wrong reason and with the wrong result. It is possible to tick the boxes that constitute formal orthodoxy but to join them up with a narrative which undermines or flatly denies what a fully biblical orthodoxy would actually affirm. That is the underlying critique, at a structural level, which I would offer of today's right-wing Christianity on both sides of the Atlantic.[14] When the fundamentalist affirms that Jesus was raised bodily from the dead, this is not normally seen as the ground for a belief in new creation, but rather simply as evidence for a dualistically conceived supernatural divine intervention, leading to the conclusion that (among other things) there really is a heaven and a hell and that one's destination is determined by one's belief. In other words, the resurrection is invoked in support of a *conservative* Platonic modernism over against a *radical* Platonic modernism. Nothing there about new heavens and new earth; nothing about the bodily resurrection of God's people to share in that new world. Likewise, when the fundamentalist declares that God will indeed judge the world, this is more likely to be conceived in terms of God blasting this wicked universe to smithereens, condemning the wicked to hell and snatching the righteous up to heaven; whereas the biblical picture, from the Psalms right through to Romans and Revelation, is of God the creator judging the creation in the sense of setting it right at last, not destroying the world of space, time and matter but administering restorative, healing justice. Fundamentalism in its various forms thus regularly shares in the gnostic worldview at a structural level even while affirming the doctrines – creation, resurrection, final judgment – which, if taken in their full biblical context, would critique it and propose the early Christian alternative.

It is to that more fully biblical narrative that we now turn, in the second part of this chapter.

Creation and new creation

One of the startling features of modern New Testament scholarship has been the relative absence of major work on the early Christian view of creation and new creation.[15] There are some significant exceptions, but they have tended to come from the margins of the mainstream discussion and have not, by and large, transformed the mood of the whole. And when we even begin to make good this deficiency, we discover that Gnosticism, ancient and modern, is confronted at every point by a theology, and a praxis, in which creation and new creation are the basis of revolutionary good news. The announcement that the creation is good, that the God who made it is good, and that this God will one day put it to rights, rescue it from its corruption and decay, and fill it with the knowledge of his glory 'as the waters cover the sea', needs to be heard once again in a way which, by and large, it has not been in the Western world and church. These are the twin doctrines of creation and judgment, which come together in the belief in resurrection. It is no accident that all three have been under sustained attack in the Western world over the last two hundred years. Nor is it an accident that the church has so often soft-pedalled all three, fitting in with the prevailing culture rather than finding fresh and creative ways to challenge it.

We begin with John. John's gospel is rooted so firmly in the story of Genesis 1 and 2 that it is hard now to imagine how any scholar could offer a gnostic interpretation or explanation of this remarkable book, as some, such as Bultmann, used to do. The prologue, with its overt and striking evocation of Genesis 1.1, is carefully balanced by chapter 20, which highlights 'the first day of the week', in other words, the starting-point of a new creation in which the old is taken up and transformed, not least by the echo of Genesis 2 as Jesus breathes into the disciples his own commissioning Spirit. John thus belongs on the map of those many Jewish texts which, following the scriptural narrative, envisage God's fresh work as the healing, not the unmaking, of the original creation.

But creation, for John, is to be understood in terms of a Christology which grows out of the Jewish wisdom tradition, cast into the tantalizing and highly evocative mode of the *logos*. The essential purpose of the prologue is to introduce Jesus in such a way that the reader knows from the outset that he embodies, incarnates, the Jewish figure of wisdom, and thereby upstages the *logos*-speculations of other contemporary philosophies. But, in announcing Jesus thus, the writer affirms the line of thought which runs back through the Wisdom of Solomon, Ben-Sira and other sources, through Proverbs 8 in particular, right back to Genesis 1 and 2. This enables John to propose (unlike much modernist would-be creational language) that the creator creates not as it were at a distance, but precisely by intimate activity *from within* creation itself. Part of the point of shaping the doctrine of creation, via the wisdom traditions, in terms of a 'word' through whom all things came into existence is to evoke passages like Isaiah 40 and 55.[16] In those passages the divine Word goes out from the transcendent creator in order to bring about a new world, not by manipulation or 'intervention' from without, but (though its source remains in the wise energy of the transcendent God) from within. The 'word' affords John, as it afforded Isaiah, a unique combination: the word of command, as in Genesis 1, but also the warm breath through which God's own life breathes into the life of the world. The world is made *fruitful* through the Word. Learning to see creation through the lens of incarnation gives the doctrine a rich suppleness which is lost when, as so often, we are faced with the crude either/or of, on the one hand, a detached God who occasionally may 'intervene' in the world and, on the other hand, a purely immanent process in which no divine power is involved.

John's gospel should not, therefore, be understood in terms of a quasi-gnostic dualism. When John says 'the world', in a negative sense, we should not understand him in terms of, say, the Platonic matter/spirit antithesis. John does not write, 'God so *hated* the world that he sent his son so that all the pre-existent sparks of light might discover their true identity and be rescued for a disembodied salvation.'[17] No: 'the world' consists of the good creation as it has been spoiled by sin and rebellion, and thence the people of Israel insofar as they have joined in the rebellion of creation.[18] And when Jesus declares to Pilate, in a passage to which we shall return in the next chapter, that his kingdom is 'not of this world', we should note that that translation has regularly obscured what the text actually said, which was *ek tou kosmou toutou*, not 'of' this world but 'from' this world. The point is that Jesus' kingdom does not *originate with* this world, certainly not with the way the world now is; but it is definitely and concretely *for* this world. That, again, is why the resurrection matters, within both the structure and the overall purpose of John's gospel.

I retain an open mind as to whether John's gospel was written to address incipient Gnosticism – not least because of the difficulty in settling the date either of the gospel or of the rise of serious Gnosticism itself. But John's gospel clearly rules out the main elements of Gnosticism. The world remains God's world, created through the Word made known as Jesus of Nazareth; or, to put it the other way round, the God who savingly addresses Israel and the world through this Word is none other than the creator God. And God's saving purpose is not to rescue people out of creation, but to renew creation itself, rescuing it, and its human inhabitants, from evil. God's people are not an elite, chosen for a privileged life in which they can escape the world and look down on everyone else (as John's gospel has often appeared to say, not least to Christians hankering after that kind of soteriology), but rather the spirit-filled and suffering agents of new creation themselves.

And though of course 'knowledge' is important within John's gospel,[19] this 'knowledge' is not a secret *gnosis* whose possessors thereby escape the world, but a faith-knowledge which commissions them to go *into* the world with the message of new creation.[20]

Much the same is true, I believe, of the writer who was once called 'the greatest of the gnostics': Paul.

The battle over the possible relationship between Paul and Gnosticism, which was still raging when I began doctoral work, was usually conducted in terms of *derivation*: did Paul derive lines of thought, poems, key technical terms, and above all theological emphases, from an incipient Gnosticism?[21] That historical battle has obscured the possibility, for which I have argued elsewhere in relation to other themes, of an analysis not of *derivation* but of *confrontation*. A parallel, to which I shall refer in the next chapter, is that Paul did not *derive* his Christology from the language and ideology of Caesar and his cult, but rather discovered that, as he derived it from his Jewish sources, he was simultaneously *confronting* imperial claims. In the same way, I suggest, Paul did not *derive* his view of the world, God, salvation or 'knowledge' from Gnosticism (whatever that might have meant in his day). Rather, he allowed his Jewish, creational theology to stand over against incipient *gnosis*.

The clearest example in the undisputed Pauline writings is 1 Corinthians 8. The letter as a whole is rooted in Genesis 1, soaked in Paul's theology of creation and new creation. This reaches full flower in the long discussion of resurrection in chapter 15, where several of the scattered earlier themes are brought together – or, to put it another way, where it becomes clear that Paul understands the apparently disparate earlier problems as manifestations of a deep misunderstanding to which a theology of bodily resurrection is the appropriate answer.[22] Within this context, we ought not to be surprised at the sharp opening to chapter 8:

When it comes to meat offered to idols, we know that 'we all
have *gnosis*'. *Gnosis* puffs you up, but love builds you up. If
someone thinks they 'know' something, they do not yet know
as they ought to know; but if someone loves God, they are
known by him.

Gnosis here is clearly a Corinthian slogan used to justify visiting pagan temples and joining in their practices. It sustains a
worldview within which (it seems) one's actions in the material world are unimportant, leaving one free to go anywhere, to
eat anything, to do what one pleases. Paul picks up the word
gnosis, addressing it in its own terms but from his Christologically
redefined Jewish base. The real *gnosis*, it seems, is not your
knowledge of God but God's knowledge of you; other claims
to possess special *gnosis* will 'puff you up' (a favourite term in
this letter), allowing you to pose as one of the elite.

Gnosis, however, is only one of the problems Paul faces
here. We should not allow this rhetorical opening flourish to
mislead us otherwise. He faces the complex, many-sided world
of ancient paganism, and is helping the church navigate the
largely uncharted waters of what it means to live as a member
of the Christ-family within that puzzling and often hostile world.
But, though his positive theological argument goes wider than
the challenge of Gnosticism, it certainly includes it. No dualism
here: 'there is no God but one'; in other words, Paul appeals to
the most basic Jewish monotheistic confession, the *Shema*. This
is explicitly *creational* monotheism, challenging Gnosticism at
the root, as is clear from his breathtaking Christological rewrit-
ing of the prayer, a move which brings him within touching
distance of John's prologue:

> For us there is one God – the Father, from whom are all things
> and we to him; and one Lord – Jesus Christ, through whom are
> all things and we through him.[23]

In other words, we not only discover Jesus at the heart of
the central confession of Jewish monotheism, but we thereby

discover the *agency* of Jesus, as God's pre-existent second self, conceived on the model of the figure of wisdom in Proverbs 8 and elsewhere. This offers the explanatory grid for understanding not only *that* the world is the creation of the one God but *how* it comes to be so, and hence how one should behave within it. As with John, the Christological character of creation undergirds the Christologically grounded new creation. And, as Paul comments wryly, not everyone has *that* bit of *gnosis* (v. 7)! And this Christologically monotheistic doctrine of creation then enables him to mount, step by step, his argument that, despite superficial similarity between gnostic freedom and Christian freedom, the differences are profound, and produce radical differences in behaviour. This then sets the tone for the rest of the letter and similar passages elsewhere.

I do not think, actually, that even an incipient Gnosticism troubled Paul very much. I see no trace of it in Galatians, Romans or the Thessalonian letters, and only a possible hint in Philippians. First Corinthians, though, indicates that if and when Paul did meet some kind of early Gnosticism, he did not *derive* his argument from it, but drew on his Jewish traditions, Christologically reinterpreted, to propose *against* it a worldview in which the created order is the good handiwork of the one God, and in which therefore salvation consists not in being rescued from creation but in being rescued from the evils – ultimately, sin and death themselves – which have defaced that creation. That is what final judgment, and resurrection itself, are all about.[24]

Matters look somewhat different in Colossians and Ephesians. (I believe that when the various 'new perspectives on Paul' have worked their way into historical exegesis, they will compel a re-evaluation of the dogma that Paul could not have written these two letters.) True, the author uses some gnostic language (*plērōma* is the normal example). But this, once more, does not mean that the theology of the letters is derived from Gnosticism.

Rather, it means if anything that these letters confront it head on. Ephesians opens with a Jewish paean of praise, echoing Genesis and Exodus, stressing that God's secret hidden purpose, so far from being to snatch people away from earth to a detached heaven, is 'to sum up all things in heaven and on earth' in Christ (1.10). This is worked out, not by the 'elite' discovering 'who they really are', but by all people discovering themselves to be 'children of wrath', in need of rescue by grace alone (2.1–10). This salvation is then to be worked out in concrete, physical ethical obedience.

Colossians emphasizes the organic harmony of creation and salvation. The poem in 1.15–20 shares with John 1 the double root of Genesis 1 and Proverbs 8. Its very structure, with its obvious parallelisms, declares that the same God is both creator and redeemer, and that redemption necessarily therefore means new creation. The poetic exploitation of possible meanings of the first word of Genesis (*bereshith*) indicates a kind of fascinated delight with the truth of creation, interpreted once more through and through Christologically.[25] Salvation, therefore, is for Colossians a matter of sharing in the death and resurrection of Jesus Christ, and working out what that means in the practice of personal and communal living. I do not think that the Colossian 'heresy', even supposing there was one, was a kind of Gnosticism. It seems, rather, to be some form of Judaism, described ironically by the author in terms of pagan religious practices.[26] But the letter as a whole, with its strongly creational basis, rules out any form of Gnosticism in any case.

The final scene of the book of Revelation, with the new Jerusalem coming down from heaven to earth, constitutes the ultimate argument against all kinds of Gnosticism.[27] The opening scenes of heavenly worship in chapters 4 and 5 reinforce the widespread early Christian reaffirmation of the Jewish doctrine of God as creator of all things, and insist that the radical infection of evil within creation does not mean that creation itself is bad, but rather that evil is an intruder whose power is broken by the victory of the lion who is also the lamb. 'Apocalyptic', here and elsewhere in the New Testament, is not a sign of cosmic dualism, but rather a mode of declaring the creator's victory over evil, resulting in new heavens and new earth.

This points us back finally to Paul, and to one of the great climaxes in his greatest letter. Romans 8.18–27 grows directly out of Paul's entire argument about God's faithfulness to his creation and to the covenant, and forms a majestic statement of the way in which God will redeem not only human beings but also the entire created order. 'The whole creation is to be set free from its bondage to decay and to share the liberty of the glory of the children of God.' No gnostic could even contemplate such a statement, which is presumably why those who have tried to understand Paul within some kind of gnostic framework (that is, at least, much Lutheran and evangelical exegesis) have ignored this passage or marginalized it. But you cannot make sense of Romans without it. This is a key moment in the biblical narrative of judgment, which, to repeat, is not about the demolition or abolition of the created order, but the *putting to rights* of the creator's good world.[28] Creation, resurrection and judgment are the triple biblical witnesses against Gnosticisms of all sorts: creation, because the gnostic insists that the god who made the world is a bad god; resurrection, because the gnostic insists that the body is bad and is to be shuffled off if true, spiritual life is to be attained; judgment, because the gnostic is not interested in sorting out the present world, but only in escaping it.

This brief survey of key moments in the New Testament shows powerfully that the early Christians were eager to affirm the goodness of creation, and to see the role of Jesus Christ in creation as a vital interpretative key to what 'creation' itself meant. Jesus, in other words, is never seen as the one who rescues *from* creation, despite the regular assumptions both of much fundamentalism on the one hand and of the newer enthusiasm for Gnosticism on the other. He is, rather, the one who rescues creation itself, and us with it.

This propels us into the third and final section of this chapter. What might happen if we took this retold biblical narrative and applied it to the issues of our day?

Against contemporary Gnosticism

The themes of the three chapters in this book interlock and interact. We shall only see the full picture when the other elements are before us. But let me begin my plea about the gospel and our culture by saying that it's time we had the courage to speak about, and live on the basis of, creation and new creation. Neither in the first century nor in the twenty-first should Christianity be thought of in terms of a private spirituality which escapes the constraints of the created order, including one's own given humanness, in the present or the future. Christianity was and is about new creation – a new creation which began when Jesus rose from the dead, which will be completed in God's new heavens and new earth, and which is glimpsed and grasped partially, but still truly, through the Spirit in the present.

What does this say about Western culture over the last two hundred years? It is routinely assumed that with the Enlightenment the world entered a new age, so that from now on everything is different, giving Western humankind a mandate to think and act differently, to set new goals and targets and use any necessary means to attain them. Part of the rhetoric of the Enlightenment has been that ordinary Christianity is based on a mistake: it is historically discredited, morally obnoxious, personally damaging, and generally not the sort of thing that sensible people would want to be associated with. And in the middle of all this we find the rejection of resurrection: not because of newly discovered historical data, or better grasp on scientific method, but because Easter offers an alternative eschatology to that of the Enlightenment. World history cannot have two decisive turning-points; the rhetoric of the Enlightenment must therefore be shored up by denying the claim of the early Christians. There are then two options: either reject the resurrection, as liberal Enlightenment thought has done, or domesticate it, as conservative Enlightenment thought has done, turning it simply into the great miracle which shows how powerful God is, or into the sign that we shall after all go to heaven when we die, or, as the last resort, into a child's happy ending to a nasty story, with eggs and bunnies to make us feel better. In both the liberal and conservative modernist readings, Gnosticism triumphs: the liberal is free to reinvent Christianity as a movement of personal self-discovery, the conservative to say 'this world is not my home; I'm just a-passing through'.

Thus Gnosticism, rejecting resurrection either wholesale or in its true meaning, cuts the nerve of the biblical themes of creation and judgment. As I said, the right-wing version emphasizes creation – but in a mechanistic, non-Christological way; and it stresses judgment – but in a destructive and punitive, not restorative, way. The left-wing version, often in reaction, follows its ancient forebears in rejecting creation and judgment altogether, only to find that there is no moral ground left to advocate justice and ecology within God's world. This leaves a moral vacuum, which is then filled with new rules, all shiny and shrill, a parody of a genuine Christian ethic.

These two types of contemporary Gnosticism generate different, and equally inadequate, readings of the gospels. In right-wing gnostic readings, found characteristically within fundamentalism and some types of evangelicalism, Jesus' announcement of God's kingdom is simply about 'going to heaven when you die', not about God's kingdom breaking in on earth as in heaven. In left-wing gnostic readings, which have elevated conspiracy theories to an art form, the canonical gospels are bravely declared to be a priori unhistorical, and in need of replacement by the gnostic gospels, whose 'Jesus' encourages his hearers to explore their own inner depths, to follow their own star, and to develop a transcendent spirituality which leaves behind the mess and muddle of the present world. I can understand why that should be popular within post-Enlightenment, and now within postmodern, culture, as it was in the confused world of the second and third centuries. But I find it hard to understand why anyone should take it seriously as a historical proposal about Jesus, or should suppose that Christianity began as a kind of gnostic spirituality and then developed into the Jewish kingdom-of-God movement we find in the synoptic traditions.

Both these options – the right and left wings of contemporary Gnosticism, if you like – leave the church in difficulties in its mission and life. If, as in Romans 8, the work of renewing creation has already begun in Jesus and is to be carried forward in the power of the Spirit, then working to protect the ecological balance in the present time is enormously and urgently important – a conclusion which is resisted tooth and nail by today's right-wing Gnostics, and which left-wing Gnostics often want to assert but without deep theological justification. Similarly, the work of restorative justice, in criminal justice systems within nations and in global issues within the worldwide community, is made far harder by the flight from creation, resurrection and judgment into various types of Gnosticism. Notoriously, right-wing Gnosticism, caring about the salvation of souls and envisaging judgment as the punishment of the unsaved along with the wicked world itself, has an easy solution to the problems of crime at the local level and problems such as terrorism at the global level: anticipate God's 'judgment' here and now, in punitive retribution. The political left has argued strongly against both, but without the theological investment that would yield a serious alternative. The theological left, embracing various kinds of neo-Gnosticisms, is regularly reduced to the impotence of postmodern sloganeering. But those who are grasped by the fresh wisdom waiting to be discovered in scripture will be able to work towards that doing of justice and mercy, and that humility in doing them, which was spoken of by the prophets and which characterizes the whole work of new creation.

One obvious, though highly contentious, area in which this applies is sex. On the right, the Gnosticism of much fundamentalism (this applies, by the way, both to Roman Catholic and to modern Protestant forms) has taught that the human body and its functions are shabby, dirty or actually evil, and this has produced a pseudo-ethic in which sexual activity, grudgingly permitted in marriage, is shunned elsewhere for all the wrong reasons. On the left, as I noted before, the implicit Gnosticism of our culture has encouraged people to look for their 'identity' deep within themselves, where they often find the spark of sexual impulse or excitement, and conclude that this 'identity' is the thing which then defines them and legitimates whatever behaviour it urges.

Over against these gnostic distortions, the story of creation, resurrection and judgment indicates well enough where the foundations for a fresh Christian sexual ethic might lie. Avoiding entirely the caricature offered by the Gnosticism of the right, it is important to reaffirm the goodness of our embodied selves, including the male-plus-female ordering of creation. The two greatest New Testament eschatological scenes employ the imagery of marriage (Revelation 21) and childbirth (Romans 8). They thus indicate at a structural level that male/female complementarity is not a mere evolutionary accident, nor something confined to the old creation, nor yet an arrangement brought about through the intrusion of evil in the world, but is woven deep into the God-given world of both creation and new creation. (To raise this question without the space to develop it in the sensitive and careful way one might wish to may be unwise, but it would be still worse to pass over in silence an area where the map I have sketched may provide some alternative routes through difficult terrain.)

I have thus come to regard the present fashion for all things gnostic (which is to be sharply distinguished from careful historical scholarship on the subject) as a bizarre and unhelpful feature of our culture, to be addressed with the good news of the Christian gospel. Whether it's *The Da Vinci Code*, or the 'new myth of Christian origins'; whether it's the attempt to suggest that this or that gnostic gospel might be worth more, historically and theologically, than the ones in the canon; whether it's the elitism of Western culture and its casual disregard for the planet and its other occupants; whether it's the deep dualism of fundamentalism; whether it's the failure of a contemporary Christian ecology; in all these ways I believe it is time to restate, and even more importantly to relive, the ancient biblical wisdom of creation, resurrection and judgment, to worship the creator God who made a good world and who will one day remake it, and to share in that project, not of escapism but of new creation, in the present time in the power of the Spirit.

Conclusion

What, then, does the Christian gospel have to say to this important feature of our contemporary culture? Equally importantly, how can it say it? (Merely to content ourselves with getting the theory right might collude with an intellectualism which is itself part of the problem.) To announce the good news that there is one God, the creator, and that this God is made known in and through Jesus Christ, crucified and risen, and that through him new creation has begun in which the present creation will be put to rights at last – this is good news indeed for those trapped within the gnostic assumptions of post-Enlightenment modernity. But it won't be much good just saying it. This message, by its very nature, can only truly be told by a community that is living by it – living, that is, in celebration of the goodness of creation without collapsing into the licentiousness which results from imagining that there is no such thing as evil within the good creation, but rather practising the self-denial which is incumbent on those who follow Jesus; living in anticipatory celebration of the new creation in which all wrongs shall be put to rights and every hurt be healed, and making that real in public, political, global and economic life as well as in personal and communal holiness. But if a community is really committed to living this way, renouncing Gnosticism and embracing creation, resurrection and judgment, it will face, as did the early Christians, the challenge of public and political life, not least the challenge of empire. And that brings us to our next chapter.

2

Jesus the Lord: the gospel and the new imperialism

One question I did not raise in Chapter 1 was why ancient Gnosticism began. Addressing that question here provides a quick and sharp introduction to our second topic.

I make no pretensions to expertise on gnostic origins. But one proposal which seems to me to have strong historical coherence goes like this. It seems quite likely that the Gnosticism we find in the late second century ad received a decisive impulse from the failure of the Jewish revolts in the 130s. Why so? Look at it like this. Suppose one were a devout Jew living in that time, pinning one's hopes on the God of the Bible acting once more within history to get rid of the hated Roman domination. Supposing you were hoping that, through the dramatic action of this God, the Jewish people would be able to rebuild the Temple and bring in God's kingdom at last, perhaps through the leadership of the 'Son of the Star', Bar-Kochba (who turned out to be the last great would-be Messiah of the period). Supposing you then managed, somehow, to survive the awful debacle of ad 135, to crawl away and lick your emotional as well as physical wounds at leisure. Might you not come to the dreadful, but coldly comforting, conclusion that the God of the Bible had led you into disaster? And – since long habits of devotion might not allow you to dispense with the text altogether – might you not then begin to read the scriptures upside down, with the villains like Cain becoming the heroes? And might the heroes, not least yhwh himself, the creator God, become the villains, from whose clutches you ought to escape into a world of spirituality, a world with no more dangerous talk of God's kingdom coming on earth as in heaven?

Like all historical hypotheses, this remains a matter of educated guesswork, but it carries a prima facie plausibility. And, whether or not this construction has any merit, it highlights the point I want to make at the start of this second chapter: that Gnosticism flourishes in a world of empire.

Each sustains the other. The empire encourages Gnosticism by creating a world where, for most people, there seems no possibility of escape from its all-conquering power, and by encouraging types of religion which offer an otherworldly escape, and therefore see no need to offer a critique of empire, still less an alternative to it. Nothing's going to change: escape into a private spirituality![1] Gnosticism then at least tacitly encourages empire, by leading its devotees into that escapist spirituality, leaving the kingdoms of the world to be divided up by others. The serious gnostic may well regard the follies and wickedness of empire as tell-tale signs of the wickedness of the created order. But such hand-wringing, while it may assuage the feelings of sorrow or even guilt at collusion, will not generate critique or revolution. Current fashion within New Testament studies often suggests that the gnostic gospels offer the truly radical alternative to the boring, conformist theology of the canonical gospels.[2] The reality is otherwise. Only in the canon do we find Jesus declaring that all authority on earth, not only in heaven, is given to him. Only in the canon do we have Caesar making a decree in Rome and the world's true Lord being born in Bethlehem. Only in the canon do we have that extraordinary Johannine scene, central to this chapter, of Jesus speaking the truth to power as he stands before Pilate on trial for his life. My opening thesis in this chapter, hooking into the first one, is therefore that Gnosticism and empire belong closely together, and that the theology of creation which provides good news for those battling with neo-Gnosticism generates also good news for those struggling within today's new imperialisms.

36

The new imperialisms

There is of course a debate as to whether what we see in today's world is really a form of empire. The hegemony wielded by the Western world, particularly by the USA as the current sole superpower, has some close affinities with earlier empires. But there are also considerable differences. The USA does not exercise direct governmental control over far-flung states in the way that, say, Queen Victoria ruled over a worldwide empire through viceroys, governors general, and other imperial officials. Nevertheless, I tend to side with those who use the word 'empire' to describe today's reality.[3] I do so not least because, as a Roman historian, I like many others observe several parallels between the Roman empire of the first century and the US empire of the twenty-first; and also because, as an Englishman, I know enough of my own country's imperial past to spot parallels there too.

This last qualification means that I do not speak from any high moral ground. I am often jealous of my Irish friends, who possess the effortless moral superiority of having been the victims of British tyranny, which then gives them an automatic affinity with the USA through the parallels between William of Orange vis-à-vis the Irish and George III vis-à-vis George Washington. But our varied backgrounds are in the last analysis beside the point. I take refuge in my primary task of history and exegesis and offer the following contemporary reflections, to which I find myself compelled at this moment in our history.

First, I offer an analysis of empire in general, and the way in which the contemporary Western empire mirrors all too closely the follies and wickednesses of its ancient archetypes. Second, I propose an analysis of the early Christian response to the Roman empire, and its fearless proclamation of Jesus as the world's rightful Lord. Third, I suggest that the Gnosticisms which have characterized both left-wing and right-wing

Christianity in our world have robbed themselves of the tools to address the problem and come up with serious alternatives. Fourth, I explore how the New Testament propels us to work for ways in which the Christian gospel may have its proper impact in proclaiming Jesus as Lord in this world of neo-imperialism.

I shall say more in Chapter 3 about the way in which the whole modernist movement we associate with the Enlightenment has increasingly given way to postmodernity, which itself belongs closely with Gnosticism and empire. Here I simply note the logic of the rise of the European empires in the eighteenth and nineteenth centuries. When you embrace the doctrine of progress and enlightenment as expounded by the philosophers of the period, empire becomes not only a possibility but an obligation. If we have attained a new level of civilization, we have a duty to share it with the world. This was exactly how the ancient Roman imperial rhetoric worked, as a glance at Cicero and similar thinkers will reveal. We Romans are naturally free; we naturally possess 'justice'; we believe in and maintain 'peace'; and this gives us an obligation to share our unique gifts with everybody else. Of course, these gifts come with a price tag, but that is only to be expected granted the great benefits that are being conferred. The British genuinely believed this rhetoric in the nineteenth century and on into living memory; I have heard it expounded, quite recently, by old India hands. In particular, the doctrine of progress, as set out by Malthus and others in the early nineteenth century, meant that a form of what would later be called 'social Darwinism' actually antedates Darwin himself, and may have provided some of the ideological conditioning which led Darwin to his biological hypotheses. Nations and societies survive and flourish, it was thought, in proportion to their fitness to do so, and the scientific and technological advances which enabled the Western powers to charge off round the world planting colonies, ruling the natives and coming home with bulging pockets, indicated well enough who was fittest, who was the global elite, who therefore had the quasi-scientific right and justification to rule large swathes of the world. (One would have thought that the twentieth century would have destroyed that particular theory, but it has proved remarkably resilient.)

Within this, the political systems that evolved in the eighteenth century have been regarded as, almost by necessity, the high point, the eschatological moment, within various doctrines of populist progress – what might be called the ideology of universal suffrage.[4] Once the divine right of kings had been scornfully rejected as an obvious power-play, 'Vox Populi, Vox Dei' provided the obvious alternative slogan, and with atheism on the increase the 'Vox Dei' bit was set aside, leaving 'Vox Populi' to become a law unto itself. If only the people's voice could be heard and harnessed, then the world would attain its long-denied utopia. Today's political puzzlements both within Europe (especially France), and between Europe and the United States, arise partly from the failure of this expectation to materialize: we have all been voting for a long time now, and utopia has failed to arrive on schedule. Modernist rhetoric has kept up the pretence for some while, suggesting that a little bit more reform, better housing and healthcare, more appropriate foreign aid, the export of democratic freedoms to other countries, and so on, will enable us to turn the corner and bring about the long-awaited perfect world at last. But part of the reason for the postmodern revolt against the doctrine of progress, not least in its political manifestations, is the recognition that this hasn't happened and isn't going to happen. This was highlighted dramatically and tragically for us by the events of the first decade of the twenty-first century, most decisively with September 11, 2001 but continuing through the tortured events (I use the phrase advisedly) that are still unfolding in the Middle East and elsewhere. The problem of evil, in short – not the philosopher's puzzle about explanation, but the

39 .

global puzzle about what to do – is the guilty secret which the rhetoric of empire seeks to hide. Vote for us, conform to our system, pay the taxes, and we will look after you. Paul had scathing words for that position in 1 Thessalonians 5: 'when they say, "Peace and Security"' – as the Romans did say to their subject peoples – 'then sudden destruction will overtake them, and there will be no escape.'

Global protection rackets can only last so long. Sooner or later there will be a day of reckoning, as the system topples under its own lazy, top-heavy weight. And though today's global empire is basically an economic one, kept in place by electronic transactions rather than viceroys on the ground, the same analysis remains true. (I originally wrote that section before the 'credit crunch' and the earthquake that ran through the financial markets in 2008. Was that the day of reckoning? Partly yes, it seems, and partly no. Governments bailed out the very rich; and the very rich, after a few moments of abject humiliation, leapt back into their private jets and carried on as before.)

Despite the economic crisis of 2008, the West still exerts an economic stranglehold over the rest of the world. Today's phenomenon of massive global debt, where the poorest countries are heavily in debt to the richest, with compound interest mounting up way above anyone's capacity to pay, is a classic example of a larger and older phenomenon, though with today's electronic efficiency we are able to escalate both the divide between rich and poor and the speed of that increase. Nor is this just about rich Westerners and poor Southerners. The line between rich and poor runs worryingly through our own cities and rural areas, producing contrasts that would take a Charles Dickens to describe properly. Furthermore, one of the main weapons of social and economic empires has always been war, both because war means subjugation of potential competitors and because war is always good business for those who supply armaments on the one hand and who rebuild bombed communities on the other. And, within this kind of imperialism, both ancient and modern, the creation itself becomes irrelevant: it is merely territory to drive tanks over, the location of resources, another piece of ground on which to plant a flag – or, as it may be, a cross – when there are rebels who need to be taught a lesson. Thus it was with ancient Rome. Thus it was with Britain in the eighteenth and nineteenth centuries. Thus it is with the Western powers today.

To be sure, solving the problem of global debt is not as easy as some cheap-and-cheerful anti-globalization protesters have imagined. It remains, however, hugely counter-intuitive (except to those completely soaked in Enlightenment elitism) to imagine that there is any justice in two-thirds of the world being head over heels in debt to the remaining one-third, with similar problems *within* nations as well as between them. The bad smell of decaying empire hangs around certain countries who boast of their large overseas aid budgets, only for it then to be revealed that at least in the recent past a large proportion of this aid has been ring-fenced for those countries to buy products we ourselves produce. Moreover (though I understand that, in the case of the UK, this has now changed), a large proportion of those products used to be guns, tanks and land-mines. War is, in fact, good for empires and good for business, and always has been. To pretend to a disinterested quest for global justice and peace while getting rich on the proceeds of war – not least, other people's wars! – is either hypocrisy or criminal blindness.

Within this neo-imperial ideology, the call to stewardship of the created order takes a back seat. Who cares about looking after the ecosystem when there are wars to be fought and money to be made? What is the point (one might ask) of everyone in the Western world religiously installing more eco-friendly light-bulbs when thousands of helicopters and bombers are polluting the atmosphere as much in one minute as such small-scale actions will improve it in a year?

But it's not just that ecology is of lesser importance. If we are the elite, and if the real God is the super-spiritual one who is only interested in heaven, not in earth – and if, as in the Cold War, this God has raised up the democratic West, particularly the USA, to keep the wicked Soviet atheists (and/or the dangerous Middle Eastern Islamists) at bay, making us the world's police force – then we have not only the right but the duty to act as masters, not stewards, of creation, making it conform to our plans and serve our divine calling. At this point the right-wing neo-Gnosticism of which I spoke in the previous chapter comes into its own. Jesus is going to return very soon, and the world is going to be no more; why worry about acid rain or nuclear fallout when you're waiting for the Rapture? Indeed, might we not be able to hurry the eschaton on its way? We thus arrive at the deeply ironic position where those most opposed to Darwinism when it's taught in school biology lessons collude with it at a much deeper level. We, the elite, the fittest to survive, can make war, make money, and make pretty much anything else we like, because we are the chosen people, with our souls secure in heaven and the world helpless at our feet.

Just as we can understand the attraction of Gnosticism in a world where people feel alienated for whatever reason, and bruised by their traditional religions, so we can see the attractions of empire. St Paul declares that all the powers in the world were created in and through and for Christ; God does not want anarchy, because then the bullies and the wicked always win at the expense of the weak and the virtuous. But, as Jewish and Christian thinkers saw and said in the ancient world, rulers and authorities always face the temptation to become bullies and wicked themselves, and they usually succumb to this temptation. That is why, after both world wars of the last century, efforts were made to create supra-national structures which would prevent such a thing happening again. And, in turn, that is why today's global empire, both in its economic form (i.e. globalized companies) and in its political form (i.e. many attitudes now endemic in the United States) so firmly resists, and indeed scorns, any structures of accountability, including now not only the United Nations but also, apparently, the Geneva Convention.

We can now observe some ways in which the new imperialism and the new Gnosticism feed off one another.

First, empires create conditions for Gnosticism, because many subjects of an empire feel alienated, outside the process, unable to alter the course of their own world. As in the Roman empire, the fact that some people at least get to vote from time to time may alter the surface texture, but it doesn't touch the deep reality of the empire which goes on its way whatever. So people retreat into private, detached spirituality. In particular, they indulge conspiracy theories about what 'they' are up to – and 'they' can be politicians, the media, the church, or indeed the Russians, the Muslims, the Chinese, anybody we choose. The idea that there is a secret knowledge out there and that one might stumble upon it and thus expose some giant conspiracy is hugely powerful, not least because sometimes, as in recent corporate scandals, it seems to be actually true.

Second, empires are happy for people to embrace Gnosticism, because the gnostic poses no threat to the empire. If religion is about me discovering my true inner self, so as to escape from the wicked world, then I have no reason to tell Caesar he is wrong about anything, and he will have no reason to be cross with me. One of the best answers to the new 'myth of Christian origins' is the fact that, in the second and third centuries, it was the orthodox, not the Gnostics, who were being thrown to the lions and burnt at the stake. This is a point that needs to be rubbed in whenever anyone says, as they frequently do, that the canonical gospels, and the portrait of Jesus they enshrine, were designed to gain power and prestige and, ultimately, social and political favouritism. Try telling that to Ignatius, Irenaeus, Cyprian or any of the Christians who lived through the great persecutions, including that of Diocletian.[5]

Third, the spin-offs of Gnosticism likewise serve the interests of empire. Religious pluralism, which Gnosticism feeds off as it gathers disparate elements of religions and cobbles together its own new constructs, means that no deity is allowed to challenge the quasi-divine empire itself (unlike classic Judaism, where the one God challenges all tyrants, and classic Christianity, where Jesus Christ is Lord of earth as well as heaven). Monotheism itself is under sustained attack as being the cause of many if not all contemporary social ills: pluralism in society seems (to some) to require pluralism in theology, and the impetus which led some in the second and third centuries to read their ancient scriptures upside down, with Cain as hero rather than villain, is being reproduced in our own day.[6] Sexual amorality, in which everyone explores and expresses what they perceive as their inner personal identity, pulls away from the strong bonds of marriage and family, sometimes indeed condemning those structures, too, as oppressive, so that identity is found either in the individual alone on the one hand or the much larger collective, the empire itself, on the other.

Fourth, within contemporary gnostic imagination there is a powerful theme which emerges, as a parody of the Christian gospel, in the myth of the superhero. Superman and his lookalikes remain hidden, just ordinary bespectacled folk, until the moment of crisis comes, whereupon the hidden identity is revealed and the hero is able to do things which ordinary mortals, the boring run-of-the-mill humans who don't have this secret identity, cannot and indeed must not. Thus, where the authorities are weak and powerless, the superhero must act outside the law, to confront the villains with redemptive violence and to restore peace and tranquillity to the community whose own law enforcement officers were incapable of doing so. This is a classic American myth, studied recently in two fascinating books by Robert Jewett and John Lawrence.[7] Tracing it first all the way from the Captain America comic strip through the Lone Ranger to Superman and the rest, the two authors then explore the myth's connections to the implicit and sometimes explicit political rhetoric that dominated the USA and the UK in the early years of the twenty-first century, as the United Nations played the part of the weak law enforcers and the Western Alliance acted outside the law to perform redemptive violence on the designated villains (in this case, Iraq).

Fifth, in all this, tragically, the church itself, not least the would-be orthodox church, all too often goes along for the ride. Precisely by insisting on a rigid church–state split, the Western church – even in countries like England where we still have an established church! – has often cut itself off from the possibility of providing an appropriate critique. Fear of the church being muzzled by the state on the one hand, and of the church gaining inappropriate power in the state on the other, have led illogically to the position where Christianity is assumed to have nothing to do with politics. In fact, the opposite is true: from very early on – from the time, in fact, when Jesus announced God's kingdom and confronted Pontius Pilate with God's claims about truth, power and kingship – the Christian faith, like its Jewish parent, has claimed the right to speak the truth to power, to call the powers of the world to account before the power of God. That, as we shall see in a moment, is part of what Paul is talking about in Colossians. It is a very considerable part of what St John is talking about in Revelation. And I suggest that our semi-gnostic propensity to concentrate on a spiritual message over against, or to the exclusion of, the claim of God on the entire creation has led us into a radical inability to say anything very much to, or about, contemporary political issues, not least because we are afraid that if we try we will be shouted down and told to go back to our real business of saving souls. Empires positively *want* churches to embrace gnostic patterns of thought and life. Then when reality reasserts itself, though now totally out of shape, the church that has been outside the political process for too long suddenly throws its weight behind this or that agenda, producing would-be holy empires in the Middle Ages, Marxist theologies of liberation in the twentieth century, and, balancing that, the newish Religious Right. Note: I am not saying that all these movements are wrong in absolutely everything they say and do. I am merely drawing attention to the fact that at the structural level they all too often exhibit the marks of a church that has forgotten the nuanced biblical roots of Christian political critique.

Anyone involved in Christian work or leadership must learn to recognize the undertow, within our whole society, of this toxic combination of Gnosticism and imperialism. Indeed, we must learn to recognize it within our own communities, our own churches, our own selves. Again, please note, I am not saying that there is no such thing as true knowledge of our selves, or indeed that there are no such things as God-given power structures. We must not in our turn become dualists, embracing a simplistic analysis which then supports a mere shrill denunciation instead of a gospel proclamation. Things are more complex than that: God does indeed raise up principalities and powers to look after his world, to bring a measure of appropriate judgment into the world in advance of that ultimate judgment which God himself will perform. That, as I suggested before, flows exactly from the doctrine of creation itself. To suggest, as some do, that we simply collapse into a politically correct left-wing anarchy is as much a denial of the doctrines of creation and judgment as it is to suggest that the powers that be are divine and can do no wrong (which is not, by the way, what Paul says in Romans 13, despite what some people have suggested).

In particular – and this is enormously important for us to grasp, not least in the church and at this time – the gospel answer to the heady combination of Gnosticism and imperialism is the combination of Christian unity and public truth. For John, in the movement from chapter 17 to chapters 18 and 19, and for Paul, in his great statement of the unity of the church in Ephesians, it is the unity of the followers of Jesus Christ which functions as a sign to the world, and to its powers, that Jesus is Lord and that they are not. It is the creation of a single new humanity in Jesus Christ which does what the empires of the world want to do but cannot do. That unity can precisely never be the anything-goes of a gnostic movement where everyone pursues their own spiritual interior pathway, but must follow the hard and high road of a unity based firmly on the public truth of the gospel. This is the difference between the Christian revelation and the gnostic claims: the Christian gospels, and the history they set before us, are a matter of public record and scrutiny, which is why the historical study of Jesus remains not only appropriate but vital. But the gnostic gospels purport to offer secret revelations for the initiate, on matters that will lead you into the private world of dualistic spirituality. Public truth for the public world; that's what the Christian gospel offers, because the risen Jesus is Lord of earth as well as heaven. And that is the answer both to Gnosticism, to imperialism, and to their potent and dangerous combination.

We desperately need this perspective if we are to keep alive our witness in the days to come. So long as we maintain the now traditional split of religion and politics, of faith and public life, of God and the world – as the gnostic ideologies of the West have done for so long that many people don't realize there is an alternative – we are powerless to do more than lament before this travesty. The good news is that in the great scriptural narrative we have for so long hushed up there is a different story, one which calls all human empires to account. This is the biblical story of the strange lordship of Jesus Christ, to which I now turn in the second part of this chapter.

Jesus as Lord

One of the extraordinary reversals in scholarship over the course of the last generation has been the rediscovery of the political dimension to the New Testament. In the 1970s hardly anyone was writing about the Roman empire in relation to early Christianity. It was assumed, partly because of the Lutheran 'two kingdoms' doctrine, coupled with the wider Western assumption of a deep split between politics and religion, that the early Christians were concerned with worshipping Jesus, living in the Spirit, being justified by faith, and explaining to one another how precisely to go to heaven, rather than with earthly politics. Paul's political views were dismissed with a wave at Romans 13. Jesus' attitude to the state was summed up in the saying about rendering to Caesar, which was taken as marking a rigid separation of powers which corresponded nicely to the modern assumption. The book of Revelation was regarded as a strange farrago of apocalyptic nightmares, which eager fundamentalists would systematize into end-times datelines and shocked liberals would dismiss as blood-thirsty fantasies. It was taken for granted that the early Christians were uninterested in serious political theology.

All that has changed in the past thirty years. In the Society of Biblical Literature, several groups have looked excitedly for critiques of empire in early Christianity. Matthew, Mark, Paul, John and especially Revelation are all deemed thoroughly counter-imperial. The pendulum has swung so far so fast that it is in danger of flying off altogether into politically driven speculations with as little historical basis as the dualism they replace. Some, indeed, retaining the dualism, now assume (ridiculously) that since the New Testament now seems to be about 'politics' it cannot after all be about 'theology'. Somewhere in the middle of all this, though, there is fresh wisdom to be found, and it comes both in the repeated assertion that Jesus is Lord – meaning, among other things, that

Caesar is not – and in the emphasis that it is *Jesus*, the crucified one, who is Lord, thereby redefining the very notion of 'lordship' itself. Of course, within many postmodern movements, not least some types of feminism, any idea of 'lordship' has been suspect *ex hypothesi*, just as any retrieval of a mainstream biblical point of view has been subject to quite fierce critique from a number of quarters. But, as I shall suggest in the next chapter, that is precisely one of the points at which postmodernity, though some of its critiques are valid, fails to deliver the goods we need and (moreover) the goods we are offered by the New Testament.

I begin, once again, with John. It has often been remarked that, whatever we think of the historical value of the rest of the gospel, the Johannine narrative of the trial before Pilate (chapters 18—19) offers a remarkably authentic picture of how a suspected rebel leader might be tried before a provincial governor.[8] But it is much more: it is the climax, within John's astonishingly skilful narrative, of the gospel-long dialogue between Jesus and 'the world',[9] and also between Jesus and his fellow Jews.[10] Pilate stands for the world, the world made by God but run by Caesar; Jesus stands for the kingdom of God, as announced by psalms and prophets, by Isaiah and Daniel.

The scene displays not just two kings but two types of kingdom. Here is Caesar's kingdom: a kingdom in which truth is relative to power (on which more in the next chapter). Jesus has come, he says, to bear witness to the truth; and Pilate's famous response, 'What is truth?', indicates the gulf between the two empires. Caesar's empire knows only the truth of Roman rule, the truth that comes out of the scabbard of a sword (or, as we would say, the barrel of a gun): the 'truth' of taxes and whips, of nails and crosses, the truth that will swap Jesus for a brigand if that's what the crowd wants, the truth that lets Pilate wriggle off one hook while impaling Jesus on another. It is the 'truth' of death, and John intends to show us that the creator God knows, and is about to enact, a deeper truth even than that. But the kingdom Jesus comes to bring is not 'from this world'. If it were, he points out, his servants would have been fighting to stop him being handed over: that's what kingdoms originating in the present world always do. This, to repeat what I said in the previous chapter, does not mean that Jesus' kingdom is a 'purely spiritual' one, a gnostic dream of escape, with nothing to do with the present world and hence no challenge to offer to Caesar. No: Jesus' kingdom does not *derive from* this world, but it is *designed for* this world. But precisely because it is the kingdom of the wise creator God who longs to heal his world, whose justice is aimed at restoration rather than punitive destruction, it can neither be advanced nor attained by the domineering, bullying, fighting kingdom-methods employed in merely earthly kingdoms. Jesus thus redefines what it means to be 'lord of the world' at the same time as he redefines, with heavy Johannine irony, what it means to be 'king of the Jews'. And the Jewish leaders, meanwhile, now with crowning irony, declare that Jesus cannot be their king, since they have 'no king but Caesar'.

In the middle of this extraordinary dialogue, Jesus says something yet more striking. Pilate has warned that he has the power to crucify or release him; Jesus comments that Pilate couldn't have this authority if it were not given him from above, so that the greater sin is ascribed to the one who handed him over – in other words, Caiaphas.[11] It is truly remarkable, in the midst of the contrast between the two types of kingdom, to find this note, which alerts us to the deeply Jewish perception – itself rooted in the doctrine of creation – that God does not want anarchy or chaos, even in the present rebellious state of the world. There must be rulers, even if they themselves are bound to be drawn from the ranks of the wicked. To have no rulers is even worse. The resulting paradox, that God-given rulers send the son of God to his undeserved death, lies close

to the heart both of the New Testament's doctrine of the principalities and powers and of its multiple interpretations of the
meaning of the cross.

Thus, when we read John's gospel as a whole, and allow the
confrontation with Pilate to shape the meaning John intends
us to find in the story of the crucifixion and resurrection, we
discover a deeper meaning to those climactic events than we
get if we treat the political build-up as mere scene-setting
for an essentially apolitical doctrine of redemption. Jesus has
come not to destroy the world but to rescue it from evil. If the
structures of human authority are part of the good creation,
the abuse of those structures constitutes a double evil. Jesus'
task, driven not by the love of power but by the power of love,
is to take the full force of that double evil upon himself, and
thereby to complete the work of redemption, just as the Father
completed the work of creation at the end of the sixth day. The
final cry from the cross in John ('It is accomplished!') resonates
all the way back to God's *finishing* of creation on the sixth
day.[12] The darkness of evening brings in the seventh day, the
day of rest, before the arrival of the eighth day, 'the first day of
the week'. This is the day in which – if we are to allow John's
massive build-up of imperial and counter-imperial themes to
resonate as far as chapter 20 – the new creation is launched.
It is the day on which Jesus prepares to ascend, like the son of
man in Daniel 7, to take his place within both heaven and earth,
to rule the world from the restored Temple, the whole united
cosmos, with a new kind of power, the transformative and healing power of suffering love.

This spectacular Johannine political theology, routinely
ignored by preachers and theologians alike, conforms closely
to what we find in the synoptics. Matthew's risen Jesus insists
that all authority in heaven *and on earth* has been given to him,
which deserves further exploration in terms of Matthew's plot
and major themes. Luke contrasts the posturing of Augustus
Caesar in Rome with the humble but decisive birth of Jesus;

then, in Acts, he describes what it means that the kingdom is indeed 'restored' to Jesus as Israel's king, and to his followers acting as his strange, suffering ambassadors. In Acts 17 we find Paul accused of heralding 'another king, namely Jesus'. The book ends with Paul in Rome itself, announcing God's kingdom and preaching Jesus Christ as Lord 'openly and un-hindered'. No first-century reader would have missed the point, which was in any case implicit in the initial Ascension narrative. Within modernism the Ascension is merely a supernatural embarrassment. But within first-century worldviews (whether those deriving from Daniel 7, or those based on Roman emperor-cult, or those like the early Christian worldviews which were rooted in the one and confronted the other) it clearly meant that Jesus was now constituted as the true, and divine, lord of the world.

Mark's political theology has been variously explored, and I simply focus on his redefinition of power in 10.35–45. James and John ask to sit at Jesus' right and left. Jesus responds that they don't know what they're talking about (though the reader will soon know, as two others end up in those positions when Jesus is at last labelled publicly as 'king of the Jews'). But then comes the great redefinition: the rulers of the earth lord it over their subjects, but with you, the greatest must be the servant, and the leader must be the slave of all – *because* 'the Son of Man came not to be served but to serve and to give his life a ransom for many'. That famous verse (10.45), drawing together Isaiah 53 and Daniel 7, is not, as it has so often been treated, a detached statement of atonement theo-logy, but is rather the clinching point in this devastatingly counter-imperial statement about power. Not that it is not about (what we have come to call) 'atonement'. Rather, it is an invitation to understand atonement itself, God's dealing on the cross with the sin of the world, as involving God's victory not so much over the world and its powers (as though God were simply another cheerful Sixties anarchist) but over the worldly *ways of* power. The powers which were created in, through and for Jesus Christ have rebelled and now themselves need to be led, beaten and bedraggled, in his triumphal procession, in order eventually to be reconciled.

That echo of Colossians 1 and 2 is deliberate, and points on now to Paul. As I said, it used to be thought that Paul was a quietist, accepting magistrates and emperors with a shrug of the shoulders. I have argued elsewhere that this is a serious misreading of Romans 13, and that Romans as a whole, and for that matter Philippians too, offers a sustained if sometimes coded challenge to the absolute rule of Caesar.[13] Think of the opening of Romans (1.1–17): Jesus, for Paul, is the anointed King, the *kyrios*, the son of God, whose 'gospel' calls the whole world to loyal obedience, and generates a world of justice, freedom and peace. Paul was able, while deriving his gospel from a Christ-shaped re-reading of psalms and prophets, to phrase it in such a way as to challenge, point by point, the normal rhetoric of Caesar's empire. When Romans 8 offers a Christian variation on the Jewish eschatological hope for the renewal of creation, it upstages the boast of Rome that, under the emperor, the world was entering a new age of fruitfulness. Philippians 2 and 3 make the same point in different though related ways. 1 Thessalonians, as we saw, mocks the normal imperial boast of 'peace and security', and in chapter 4 provides a picture of the *parousia* of Jesus which seems designed to upstage the regular imperial panoply of the *parousia* of Caesar, 'arriving' at a city, or back in Rome after some great exploit, with the grateful citizens going out to meet him and escort him into the city. Regrettably, 1 Thessalonians 4 has become notorious as the proof-text for a 'rapture' in which God's people will be snatched away from earth to heaven, leaving them without the promised new heavens and new earth, and leaving Paul without one of his more powerful pieces of anti-Caesar rhetoric. This is a tell-tale sign of the underlying Gnosticism which eats away at the gospel from within, leaving the contemporary church less able to mount its own critique of empire.

Central to Paul, of course, as to John and Mark, is the theology of the cross, which is again to be seen not only in terms of traditional 'atonement' theology but also in terms of counter-imperial polemic. As any student of Roman history knows only too well, crucifixion was not just a very nasty mode of execution but also a clear statement of power. It warned subject peoples, slaves and insurgents that Rome ruled the world, that Caesar was Lord, and that resistance was both futile and very, very foolish. It made, already, the theological point that the goddess Roma ran the world, and required her subjects – especially in the Middle East which supplied the grain essential to the well-being of the overcrowded city of Rome itself – to do what they were told when they were told. It took not only genius but considerable chutzpah to see, and to say, that the symbol which spoke of the horrible 'justice' of Caesar's empire could now speak of the restorative justice of the true God. All this is based on the resurrection: if death is the ultimate weapon of the tyrant, then resurrection is the reassertion that the creator God rules over the world which the tyrants claim as their own. (This means, by the way, that denying the resurrection is a way of colluding with imperial power, which reminds us again why that denial was so important within Enlightenment thought, as indeed within second- and third-century Gnosticism.) While in itself high-lighting one of the majestic truths at the heart of the Christian faith ('the Son of God loved *me* and gave himself for me'[14]), to speak only of 'atonement' in the dehistoricized and depoliticized sense of 'Christ dying for my sins' as a kind of private transaction is to run the risk once more of colluding, gnostic-fashion, with empire, implying that the redemption I enjoy will enable me to leave behind for ever the world where imperial powers continue to behave as they always do. Sadly, some who have insisted on speaking only of the personal meaning of the cross do seem to have that as part of their agenda. Equally, to imagine that we can reduce Matthew, Mark, Luke, John or Paul to terms simply of 'politics', as though their political stance is not rooted in their theology of creation, atonement and new creation, is to reduce them to echoes of our own largely impotent political posturing.

It is the underlying theology, in fact, which enables the New Testament writers to avoid that kind of shallowness and lay the foundations for a mature political theology. We trace their thinking, through books such as the Wisdom of Solomon, all the way back to the biblical story of God's people under pagan rule. The line from Genesis 3 to the Tower of Babel in Genesis 11 then gives way to the call of Abraham; Abraham's family ends up in Egypt, rescued when God judges their pagan overlords; the deeply ambiguous conquest of Canaan results in the still ambiguous kingdom of David and Solomon; and eventually we find ourselves back in Babel, in the Babylonian exile which creates the context for those two most deeply political prophecies, Isaiah and Daniel. All through this story (and probably shaped by this last experience) we find the large implicit question of the relationship between Israel as the people of the creator God and the powerful empires of the world. The Psalms, meanwhile, celebrate the kingship of yhwh over the nations, and yhwh's placing of his Messiah as the one who will bring the kings of the earth to order – while almost as often complaining that this wonderful plan doesn't seem to be working out too well. Subsequent Jewish retrievals of this massive narrative of God and the nations form a fascinating topic for another time.[15] Sufficient to note that this story formed the matrix within which the early Christians fashioned their own political stance.

At the heart of this stance we find the affirmation, the good news: Jesus is Lord. *Jesus*, the crucified one, is Lord; not another Caesar to bully and threaten, but the one whose life and death redefined power for ever. The book of Revelation is now widely and correctly seen as one of the great documents of early Christian political theology, offering a further account of the victory of the creator God over the rebel powers of the world, a victory rooted in God's determination to restore and fulfil the creational intent and accomplished through the self-giving death of the Lamb. Revelation joins the rest of early Christianity in announcing that Jesus is Lord of earth as well as heaven, and that at his name every knee shall bow. This constitutes very *bad* news to relativists, ancient and modern; and relativism, like the Gnosticism which often employs it, regularly accompanies empire, since, as we shall see in the next chapter, those for whom there are no ultimate truths will have difficulty undermining the truth-claims of empire. But the objection of the relativist is met by the redefinition of power at the heart of the gospel. It is the wrath of the *Lamb* that deals with all that defaces God's creation. John's Jesus comes not to condemn but to rescue. His rule is not about power as we know it, but, once more, about the power of love.

The Lordship of Jesus, the central topic of this chapter, is thus to be understood in harmony with the previous one, the creation and judgment which constitute the good news over against the dark world of Gnosticism. Jesus' Lordship is not outside, or over against, the restorative purposes of the creator God. Rather, he is exalted through his resurrection and ascension to the place where the God who made the world through him now rules the world through him. As Paul says, quoting Isaiah 11 at the final climax of his greatest letter, Jesus is the one 'who rises to rule the nations; and in him the nations shall hope'.[16] Only those who have lived with the hopelessness of human empire will fully appreciate that promise, just as only those who have lived with the violence of empire will fully appreciate the meaning of the victory over violence itself won on the cross.

The New Testament's theology of creation, resurrection and new creation thus not only provide good news for those sunk in the dualism of Gnosticism. They form the solid platform for the central gospel assertion that Jesus Christ is Lord, the good news for those in a newly imperial world. The good news is that this Lordship is not a mere heavenly lordship, distracting attention (and critique) from the tyrannies of the world. The lordship of Jesus is designed for earth as well as heaven, both in the ultimate future when heaven and earth are one and in the penultimate future, in which he died and rose again in real space, real time and a real body, and in which his followers work to bring signs of his healing and hopeful rule to birth in the present time. It is to this task, difficult and complicated though it may seem, that we now turn in the third section of this chapter.

Living in God's alternative empire

The last decade has forcibly reopened the question many in our world had considered closed for ever, that of the interrelation of faith and public life. It had never really gone away, of course, but for much of the last two centuries, on both sides of the Atlantic, it has been regarded as effectively off limits. I have noticed that in the USA the idea that church and state might have anything to do with each other is often attacked with real venom, perhaps again with long memories of George III sending bishops to the colonies. In the UK, as well, there is an increasing clamour from the press and from some politicians for a complete separation, for the ancient links of church and state to be broken at last. Now, with the proliferation of multi-faith communities in many formerly monochrome parts of the world, and particularly with the rise of a militant Islam, we face old questions in new ways.[17]

Some, predictably, have continued to give the same old secularist answers, only now in a shriller tone. In the UK all kinds of controversies have arisen, from a moderate politician who said that he preferred Muslim women in his constituency to

57

take off their veils when they came to see him to the national airline that tried to sack a black Christian woman for wearing a cross while on duty. Our national broadcasting organization raised similar objections about a cross worn by a newsreader. (At least, we might reflect, that shows that the cross-as-decorative-jewellery, so long a 'sleeping' signpost to some kind of Christian faith, is capable of waking up quite suddenly.) Politicians and columnists to left, right and centre have chipped in with comments which indicate that we are totally unused to addressing questions of religion, culture and public life, and unaware that there might be some old maps to help us find our way through countryside which is virgin territory to us but which was well known to many of our forebears in all the great world faiths.

This, like September 11, 2001 itself, is one of those postmodern moments which reveal all too clearly the inadequacy of the modernist settlement to see us forwards into the twenty-first century. Religion of all sorts is back on the agenda, back in the public square; the genie is out of the bottle, and won't be forced back in again. Empires, as I said before, characteristically like pluralism and relativism: if there are many gods, none of them is likely to challenge the ruling ideology. Ever since Constantine the church has faced the temptation to work its way into a kind of power which falsifies the kind of power exercised through the cross. But the irony today is not so much that we are faced with a would-be Christian empire. It is that we are faced with an empire which, because of its Enlightenment roots, officially professes no religion; and yet routinely appeals to, and is kept in power by, certain varieties of essentially modern – and in some cases gnostic – Christianity. How can the early Christian political theology I have been exploring help us to think afresh about all of this, and navigate our way through this complex and dangerous territory?

There is a line of biblical theology which runs from Genesis and Exodus, through the ambiguous narratives of conquest and monarchy, through Isaiah and Daniel, through, indeed, the Maccabean literature and the Wisdom of Solomon, and out with a new focus into John, the Synoptics, Paul and Revelation – and for that matter Ignatius of Antioch, Polycarp of Smyrna and Irenaeus of Lyons. This biblical theology approaches questions of earthly power and the kingdom of God through the doctrines of the good creation, the promised new creation, and the lordship of the crucified, risen and ascended Jesus. We are therefore invited today to a massive task of retrieval, in implicit dialogue with political theologians of all sorts, but for which there is at the moment, as the reader may be relieved to discover, only space for a short summary.

As I said before, it is part of the doctrine of creation that the creator intends the world to be ordered and structured, with a harmony of its parts which enables flourishing, fruitfulness and the eventual fulfilment of the creator's intention. From the beginning, according to the ancient poetic story, the creator God gave to humans the task of reflecting the divine image into the world, of being the bridge between the creator and the creation, of representing the presence of God within the creation and the presence of creation before God, and of doing so with a rich awareness, a thoughtful appreciation, of both elements. The risk that the human race would rebel, and set up on their own, is a point in Genesis 1 which resonates deeply with several subsequent layers of the story: because, when evil enters the world, the creator does not abandon it to chaos, does not unmake creation itself, but works from within to produce an eventual restoration. Since by a man came death, by a man has come also the resurrection of the dead.

It gradually emerges, throughout the Hebrew and Aramaic scriptures, that part of this divine purpose is to call and equip rulers, not only within Israel itself but within the pagan nations of the wider world, to bring a measure of order to the world – and even sometimes, as in Isaiah 10, to bring judgment upon God's people! Those rulers themselves remain part of the problem. They abuse their vocation, and further their own ambitions of violence, greed and hollow glory. The ambiguity of human power – the necessity of it on the one hand, and the inevitable temptations of it on the other – thus flesh out the precarious position of the humans at the beginning and also of Israel as the story develops. The Israelites, called like Adam and Eve to a specific role within the creator's purposes, rebel like Adam and Eve (that may be part of the point of the way the story came to be told), and are eventually ejected from the garden, the promised land. The promises to which Israel clung over the following centuries combined the two elements which give shape to early Christian political thought as well: first, God's use of non-Jewish powers to restore and give order and security to the post-exilic community; second, God's challenge to those very powers (and God's promise to the chosen people) that the coming Messiah, and/or the messianic community, would eventually put the whole world to rights, which would involve the demotion of all powers from the proud, arrogated position they routinely occupy.

Let me put it like this, in a threefold typology, based on the doctrines of creation and redemption.

1 God intends the world to be ordered, and will put it in proper order at the last; but
2 he doesn't want chaos between now and then, and uses human authorities, even when they don't acknowledge him, to bring a measure of his order in advance of the end; and
3 since that puts authorities in the position of awful temptations, God's people have the vital calling to speak the truth to them and call them to account in anticipation of that same final day.

I hope it is clear that this gives to second-Temple Jewish thought, and thereby to early Christian thought, a complexity and density which does not correspond to the over-simple political alternatives familiar in today's Western world. (Many debates today, including debates about the political thought of the early church, are still conducted within the post-eighteenth century Western framework of an easily grasped left/right spectrum, which functions as a Procrustean bed when it comes to the much more complex and nuanced viewpoints of first-century Jews or Christians, or for that matter pagans.) Perhaps it is also clear that this complexity corresponds much more to the way many other people in today's world see public life, and that if we are to engage with the world we live in, instead of assuming that our post-Enlightenment political mindsets are automatically superior, we would do well to think the matter through more fully. We Westerners need to beware of the political equivalent of the traditional Englishman's behaviour abroad: if the natives don't understand what you say, just speak louder.

The early Christian political theology includes the application to power of the achievement of Jesus Christ in his death and resurrection.[18] Dealing with evil within the world cannot be reduced to dealing with individual human sin, hugely important though sin and forgiveness are. It includes, and the evangelists and apostles knew it included, the victory by the creator God over all the powers that have rebelled within the world, and hence the announcement to the principalities and powers that their time is up, that Jesus is Lord and that they are not. (That is the message of Ephesians 3.10: the revelation of God's many-coloured wisdom to the rulers and authorities.) The rulers are therefore to be summoned to obedience to the Prince of Peace. The church was from the beginning entrusted with this dangerous message, and necessarily and inevitably suffered for it, but went on claiming, as in Acts, the moral and political high ground of reminding the authorities what their job really was, and holding them to it. The apostles found far less difficulty than we do in holding all this together. (I mean, intellectual difficulty; it was undoubtedly extremely difficult personally, socially, culturally and politically.) We, who have inherited the post-Enlightenment antithesis of anarchy and tyranny and have turned it into two-party systems of left and right, are called to relearn the more subtle, and more useful, biblical analysis of how the rule of Jesus Christ impacts upon the kingdoms of the world.

The church is therefore called to reject both tyranny – all rulers must bow before Jesus! – and also the anarchist dream of no powers, no 'order', no structure to God's world. Even in the promised new heavens and new earth there will be order within the promised equality; how much more, within the present world where evil still infects the human race, is it necessary that there be rulers and authorities who can hold it in check. Equally, the church must also reject the Marxist dream of a simple inversion of power, of the rule of the previous under-class but by the same means as before. Rather, the church must affirm that the creator God intends the world to be ruled by properly constituted authorities, but insists that they be held to account, and that it is part of the task of the church to do this, to speak the truth to power, to affirm power in its proper use and to critique it in its regular abuse.

Here, I think, we in the Western world have been too in love with our own modernist democratic processes, and have imagined that the only really important thing about power is how people attain it, since 'Vox Populi' will give them then the absolute right to do what they want after being elected. Part of our difficulty today is precisely that this implicit belief is held so strongly that the idea of a democratic 'mandate' is, for many, part of an unchallengeable worldview. Far too much weight then attaches to all the expensive fuss and bother about elections. Americans may like to be reminded that the rest of the world looks on in a mixture of horror and dismay at the time taken, and the inward-looking attitudes revealed, every fourth year. The de facto role of the USA in the rest of the world makes everybody else resent the fact that, during that time, global issues are framed in terms of how this or that way forward may affect the forthcoming election. Since much of the world is dependent on the USA in some respects at least, there might even be an argument that the rest of us should be voting in those elections anyway. But the early Christians, like the Jews of the same period, were not particularly interested in how someone, or some system, came to power. Nobody in the early church campaigned for more democracy, for an extension of the franchise; nobody would have imagined that, if such things had come to pass, justice and peace would have broken out at once. Rome had been holding elections for many centuries, and that hadn't prevented major problems, ending with the bloody and bitter civil wars in the second half of the first century bc.

No: the early Christians (and the Jews of the same period) did not worry too much about how people came to power. Rather, the early Christians were much more interested in what people did with power once they had it, and in holding up a mirror to power, like Daniel with Nebuchadnezzar or Darius, so that those in power might be reminded that they were responsible to the creator God and that, ultimately, they were called to bow the knee to Jesus as Lord.

If the church could recapture this vision, there might emerge a more mature political theology which would avoid the sterile left/right polarization that has increasingly characterized the USA, and the equally sterile centre/centre polarization (if that isn't too paradoxical) that has characterized the UK. Our political discourses have become shallow and naive, following the postmodern fashion for spin and smear, and appealing to social and cultural feeling rather than to genuine issues of justice, power and freedom. The church is called to bear witness, over against the prevailing Gnosticisms which have hampered our witness before the powers, to the promise of new heavens and new earth in which justice will dwell. We must refuse to be conned by the rhetoric of either the new right or the new left, and must insist on bringing signs of that future to birth both in our own lives and in the world around, based on the resurrection of Jesus and the power of the spirit.

The church must, in short, learn from Jesus before Pilate how to speak the truth *to* power rather than *for* power or merely *against* power. (I am very puzzled by the suggestion sometimes put forward that 'speaking the truth to power' might be something only established churches could really do. A great many Christians from a great many churches are doing it all the time, and many of them are suffering for it. Where the power in question is today's rampant and all-conquering secularism, as in some university cultures, it is the more necessary to stand for Christian faith and truth against a powerful rising tide.) This needs working out, of course, in economics both local and global; in ecology and stewardship of the whole creation; and, not least, in structures of global governance. The suspicion or downright rejection of the United Nations on the part of the new right – held more securely in place by the Gnosticism of the 'Left Behind' series in which the black General Secretary of the UN turns out to be the antichrist! – must be rejected if we are to become mature and genuinely work for justice and peace across the globe. Neither the USA nor the UK, nor some combination of the two, can ever again as they stand function as a credible global police force, especially in the Middle East. Yet some kind of transnational policing is necessary in some parts of the world, and if the UN can't provide it we must find ways of enabling it to do so. That is the context, incidentally, in which I find I cannot be a full-blown pacifist. Within the world the way it is, some policing will always be necessary; policing will sometimes involve restraint; restraint will sometimes involve violence. Not to admit this is to risk colluding with the bullies who are waiting in the wings for good people to remove controls. All this is just one example of the kind of fresh thinking we urgently need and which the church should be advocating.

I have been trying to explore what it might mean to live under the Lordship of Jesus Christ as Lord of earth and not just of heaven. But this begs the huge question, which will already be obvious to many: how can we speak of Jesus as Lord when all lordships are suspect? How can we speak the truth to power when truth turns out to be a function of power? How, in other words, can we work out what the doctrines of creation and the Lordship of Jesus might mean in a world of postmodernity? What does it mean to speak, in that context, of the Spirit of Truth, and of being led into all truth? To address that question is the task of the third chapter in this book.

3

Spirit of Truth in a postmodern world

The central question of our time, behind both the flight to *gnosis* and the lurch towards empire, is that of truth. It also happens to be a central question of Christian theology, including political theology. In answer to Pilate's question, 'Are you a king?', Jesus responds, 'You use that word for me; the reason I was born, and the reason I have come into the world, is that I should bear witness to the truth.' And Pilate, famously, asks, 'What is truth?'[1]

It's easy to see why. Once you deconstruct truth, it is impossible for anyone to speak the truth to power. Indeed, truth becomes merely a function of power, as Nietzsche, almost equally famously, asserted over a century ago. The parallel between Nietzsche and Pilate alerts us to the point that the central claim of postmodernity is substantially similar, and arises for similar reasons, to that of the Cynics in the centuries surrounding the time of Jesus. Faced with the rise of empires from Alexander to Augustus and beyond, the Cynics – their name means 'dogs' in Greek – barked at the posturing and pretension of the emperors, and deliberately lived, in the phrase made famous by Dominic Crossan (though he applied it to the first followers of Jesus), as 'hippies in a world of Augustan yuppies'.[2] Similarly, postmodernity has grown up in the wake of the tyrannies of the first half of the twentieth century and the increasing disquiet felt by many analysts in the Western world with the democracies of the second half. It stands on the shoulders of the seminal statements like that of Adorno, that one cannot write poetry after Auschwitz. It mocks the pretensions, especially the political pretensions, of the great modernist project of the last two hundred years. Its negative impact has quite a lot in common with the dark dualism of the gnostic view of the world, though it cheerfully deconstructs the gnostic claim to have discovered a true inner identity, let alone a true spiritual destiny. And, though some are already saying that today's young people are bored with postmodernity and want to move on, particularly to reinhabit rich and creative human relationships – which has to be a very good sign, if it's true – the postmodern movement, especially its hermeneutic of suspicion, is firmly entrenched in everything from architecture to the cinema, from journalism to sport, from biblical studies to ethnography. Right across the English-speaking world and in many other places too, there is a pervasive climate of suspicion. Whatever anyone says we will distrust it. What is truth? How might we know?

Into that situation, which I shall describe presently in a little more detail, there comes again the word from John's gospel, the word which speaks of witnessing to the truth, and of that witness somehow constituting the central feature of the 'kingdom' which Jesus came to bring, the kingdom not *from* this world but certainly *for* this world. 'You will know the truth', he had said earlier, 'and the truth will set you free'. And, in a much-quoted verse, Jesus promised that he would send his followers 'the Spirit of Truth' who would 'lead them into all truth'. The question of this chapter is therefore: how can we claim this promise within a world where all truth is suspect – the postmodern world in which we all live whether we like it or not? What impact will this have on the world we have looked at in Chapters 1 and 2, the world of a revived Gnosticism and a renewed imperialism? What does the gospel say to our complex culture?

The postmodern challenge

I have written at length elsewhere about postmodernity, and merely sum up the relevant points here. Postmodernity offers its own critique of power structures and escape mechanisms. To the empire it insists that the great story of imperial success, the empire's *Heilsgeschichte* climaxing in the Enlightenment and its fruits, is a self-serving and power-grabbing narrative. There are plenty of signs that the analysis is on target. To those who offer their supposedly scientific analyses of economic and political reality, postmodernity insists that all claims to truth are likewise claims to power, and as such are suspect. To those who seek their own identity, whether the successful identity of the self-made Enlightenment pioneer or the hidden identity of the gnostic escapist, postmodernity insists that identity, too, deconstructs. Full-on postmodernity is no friend of Gnosticism or empire. Indeed, as I have argued elsewhere, postmodernity seems within the providence of God to have the role of preaching the doctrine of the Fall to arrogant modernity.

And yet postmodernity helps create the climate within which *Da Vinci Code*-style theology can flourish. The hermeneutic of suspicion is indiscriminate, and one of its prime targets is the church itself, especially an institutionalized or established church, or a gospel in which Jesus did actually rise from the dead and is therefore the Lord of the world, at whose name every knee, especially that of Caesar, must one day bow. Postmodernity, precisely by blurring all the lines of the great stories and the great truth-claims, helps from its own angle to sustain the same religious pluralism and sexual amorality which are engendered by Gnosticism, and which empires are always happy to encourage. That is why, as several thinkers have pointed out, and as we shall see more fully in a moment, postmodernity cannot actually mount a successful challenge to empire. It can make a lot of noise, and quite a lot of that noise is noise a biblical Christian ought to agree with, since the role of postmodernity, as we just said, is to preach the Fall, and original sin, to the modernist arrogance which thinks it has evil beaten once and for all. But the empire can make plenty of noise itself, and can drown out most voices raised against it. And if postmodernity deconstructs the Christian's statements of public truth, we are left once again with no alternative but the hidden revelations and conspiracy theories of Gnosticism.

When it comes to considering empire, postmodernity ironically reinscribes the power of empire by insisting that power is all that there is. If that is so, they say, why then let's make sure it is we who wield it, and wield it effectively. And when postmodernity runs its hermeneutic of suspicion against the orthodox church itself, as we have seen happen at several levels simultaneously within our culture, then it merely opens the way once more for the proponents of Gnosticism to flourish, offering their secret alternative spirituality to those who have been bruised by the church when it has ordered its life otherwise than after the model of the good shepherd who deals gently with sheep and lambs alike.

Once again, our culture finds itself pulled and pushed this way and that by what pass for spirituality and morality at the intersection of these powerful subcurrents. There is room for a whole other book at this point, but let me just summarize. When it comes to spirituality, Gnosticism recommends following your own star; and postmodernity will agree – as long as the star can change from time to time. When it comes to morality, the one thing we all learn to criticize is power, but we don't know what to do about it. The single piece of moral high ground is that of being a victim, whether real or imaginary. And the main moral imperative within postmodernity is to embrace 'the other', that which is different from ourselves – often without realizing that 'tolerance' is not a specifically Christian position, but is rather an Enlightenment virtue, which itself sustains the all-embracing empire. These values, if that is what they are, are routinely appealed to in public life and in the church itself without any apparent awareness that they too have a history, that this history is severely constrained and conditioned by several powerful cultural forces including those

I have sketched, and that they are at best but a pale shadow of the values generated and sustained by the Christian gospel, and at worst in direct opposition to them. These postmodern values do not represent a fresh word from God, but rather the resolute determination to follow the ant in front, even if it be to death by starvation.

With these preliminary reflections, let me now say three things in particular about postmodernity. First, postmodernity tells us some things we badly need to hear, and until we've heard them we can't move forwards. Second, however, postmodernity remains impotent in its critique of the large narratives of power by which the modern world has constructed itself; in other words, postmodernity can sneer at empire but can't stop it. Third, when we see the postmodern question about truth through the lens of the conversation between Jesus and Pilate, we glimpse a new kind of answer: an answer rooted in the Trinitarian wisdom of the ancient church, and offering good news, not by going back to modernism after all, but by going on to fresh understandings of the truth-telling task of the gospel in the world. This third chapter, therefore, joins up with the previous two, attempting to present a single integrated vision of the gospel in contemporary culture.

The story of the postmodern turn is well enough known. Modernism, the great cultural movement launched by the Enlightenment, has lived on a fourfold worldview:

1 God is either an absentee landlord, or simply an absentee; religion and spirituality are private matters, irrelevant in practice and essentially escapist.
2 The world is full of facts we can know objectively, enabling us to get about and do things, make things, organize things and (especially) run things.
3 'I', the great Enlightenment individual, am the master of my fate, the captain of my soul, able to make decisions, attain personal fulfilment and stride through the world sorting it out.

4 I live in a world where the human race has come of age, has attained enlightenment through science, technology and modern democracy: a world, in other words, which has progressed beyond the infantile state of superstition we now sneer at as 'medieval', though in fact it seems to have lasted right up to the middle of the eighteenth century. In particular, I have got rid of that nasty religion business which always threatened to stop me doing what I wanted.

The first three of these – the view of God, the world, and the individual – have clear correlates within the church's self-perception over the same period. God is distant, and if we are to have contact with him we will need either an escapist spirituality for us to get in touch with him, or his 'intervention', through miraculous and supernatural deeds, into our world (where he is normally not present). We can, however, know our true Christian doctrines with a modernist, rationalistic certainty, proving God's existence, and even Jesus' resurrection, to our own satisfaction at least, in much the same way as the mathematician proves a theorem. And everything is focused on the individual, whose state of sin or grace, whose righteousness in the present and salvation in the future, is the be-all and end-all of the whole story. Fundamentalism thus grows out of the Enlightenment to the right just as modernist liberalism grows out of it to the left. As we saw, both routes lead towards the gnostic possibility and the imperial obligation. If we are in command of the facts, then we are in command.

That is what Nietzsche saw with such prescience a century or so before it became common coin within postmodernity. What is this 'truth' all about? It is simply a claim to power. The postmodern deconstruction grows from within empire, either as an impotent shout of rage or as a shoulder-shrugging collusion, which is the second point I shall come to presently. But the first point is this. Postmodernity is the necessary answer to the arrogance of modernity, the reminder of what modernity was always in danger of forgetting: there is such a thing as evil, and it has not been banished by the modernist achievements, for all that science and technology have made human life less miserable in some ways (though more so in others) and for all that democracy has enabled millions to grow up politically. (Let me just add, in case there is any confusion on the point, that I regard the Enlightenment as having conferred great blessings on the world as well as having inflicted great ills and dangerous misunderstandings.) The catastrophic events of the twentieth century, many of them directly traceable to elements within Enlightenment modernity – the First World War with its social-Darwinian legitimation on both sides, the Gulag with its relentlessly modernist atheistic ideology, the Holocaust with its determination to banish the rumour of God represented by the Jews – call sharply into question, and rightly so, the proud boast of the Enlightenment to know the truth and to be thereby set free. The objective 'knowing' propounded by the Enlightenment turns out to be the will to power, and its 'freedom' turns out to be the rampant licence of the bull in the china shop. And if the postmodern protest has had to dismantle the very categories of 'knowing', 'truth' and 'freedom' in order to make the point that modernity was guilty of massive hubris, so be it. Thus the fact of September 11, of high-tech machines flying into massive towers which spoke of the modern Western dominance of a global financial empire, constituted a literal deconstruction to match, at the level of symbol and ideology, the metaphysical deconstructions offered by Jacques Derrida, Jean-François Lyotard and the rest. The utter horrible wickedness of the act does not undermine its potency as an index of the dangerous moment our culture has reached.

But if my first point is that postmodernity has been a necessary protest against modernist arrogance, my second is that it has not provided us with an alternative worldview capable of sustaining a new way of being human in our late-modern Western world. Its view of God, insofar as it has one, is confused, opening the door to all kinds of romantic, New Age, gnostic and other theologies in which functional atheism in some quarters blends effortlessly with elements both of pantheistic mysticism and gnostic escapism. Its view of the world, following the demolition of objective truth, is likewise confused, since our relentless suspicion of one another makes us demand more and more checking up on each other, more and more 'truth' in that sense, while simultaneously reducing truth itself to spin, smear and supposition.[3] Conspiracy theories abound, as we saw in Chapter 1. And, notoriously, the 'I', the lonely Enlightenment ego, collapses into a shifting mass of signifiers, where one can choose to be somebody different every day of the week, not least by means of the internet and virtual reality machines. Thus the gnostic imperative within postmodernity echoes Oscar Wilde's sardonic comment about a cigarette: it is exquisite, but leaves you unsatisfied. The traditional 'self' is gone, but the fascinating narcissism of the search for a deeper and deeper 'personal identity' is bound to end, like *The Da Vinci Code*, in puzzlement. Maybe there never was a holy grail, a 'true self', in the first place. And postmodernity's deconstruction of the big stories, the grand narratives of progress, leads to a sharp critique of human empire, especially Western empire, which, as I said, mirrors the protest of the ancient Cynics.

But – my second point about postmodernity – though the contemporary cynics can sneer and scoff at empire, they cannot stop it in its tracks. This is strikingly argued by the Roman Catholic Cambridge scholar Nicholas Boyle in his famous book *Who Are We Now?*.[4] It is not simply that postmodernity is itself, ironically, an elitist and intellectual movement, largely ignored by the great majority of voters in Western countries, let alone elsewhere around the world, and hence having little effect not only on oligarchies and tyrants but also on the democratic process itself. It is, rather, that once postmodernity has deconstructed truth itself, it has rendered itself incapable of speaking truth to power. If all truth-statements are power-statements, the attempt to point out the failings and dangers of empire, to unmask the spin and lies by which people attain power and sustain themselves in it, is itself easily deconstructed. Empires themselves can easily co-opt postmodern techniques to brush off challenges: 'Global warming? You only say that because you're relying on science, which we know is Darwinian and anti-Christian' (I have had that one said to me), or 'Problems about global debt? You only say that because you're an anti-American crypto-Marxist' (I've had that too). 'Problems in Iraq or Afghanistan? You only say that because you're abandoning the righteous struggle of those who love freedom against those who love hatred.' (Most readers will be able to supply the footnote to that one.)

In fact, postmodern deconstruction, while it emerges in various cultures, as it has in ours, in terms of criticism of ruling ideologies, not only cannot sustain the critique but also appears, in the long run, to be itself part of the means by which empires stay in power. 'What is truth?' is precisely the question asked. Yet it is not the question Jesus asks Pilate, as though to demolish Caesar's proud empire with a strategic metaphysical outflanking. It is the question Pilate asks Jesus, seeking to ward off the challenge of a different kind of empire, an empire claiming to originate not in this world but elsewhere, an empire whose king has come to bear witness to truth itself, and thereby to offer a freedom that Caesar could never imagine. And this leads us back to where we started, to explore the notion of 'truth' within the New Testament, especially in the gospel of John.

Spirit of Truth: the witness of John

Truth is not such a widespread biblical theme as 'knowledge' or 'kingdom', though where it occurs it remains important. For Paul, God's truth is seen in creation, though it is suppressed when humans worship idols instead of God, resulting in the fracturing of their image-bearing capacity.[5] In Galatians, Paul speaks passionately about 'the truth of the gospel', the truth that in Christ God is reconciling all humans, bringing together Jew and Gentile into one family on the basis of the accomplishment of Jesus, a family characterized by nothing more nor less than faith in what this Jesus has done.[6] Elsewhere, Paul speaks of a special kind of knowing which transcends that which is available to others. This is not, however, a gnostic 'knowing' which enables one to be puffed up as part of an elite, coming to know that which was true of oneself all along, but (in his sense) a spiritual 'knowing' of the free gifts of God.[7] Paul writes about 'speaking the truth' in a way which indicates that he recognizes the dangers and pitfalls, but also the non-negotiable obligation, of trying to do so.[8]

But it is in John that the theme of 'truth' comes to fullest early Christian expression. 'The Word became flesh, and dwelt among us, and we beheld his glory, glory as of the father's only son, full of grace and truth . . . The Law was given through Moses; grace and truth came through Jesus Christ.'[9] That repeated doublet, grace and truth, invites a moment's extra thought. John has just said that the world didn't know the Word, though he was the one through whom it came into existence, and that the Jewish people didn't receive him though they were his own people. For truth to be unveiled, therefore, there must be an act of grace: there is no elite, no group within the world who merely need to have their attention drawn to what was true of them already. Only where there is this act of grace can truth be glimpsed, as blind eyes and unready hearts are enabled to see and know the truth which is revealed in and through the Word made flesh.

In particular, the Johannine prologue, as we saw in Chapter 2, deliberately roots the gospel in the Genesis creation narrative. This enables him to insist that what is accomplished through Jesus is the new creation, through which the old creation finds its true fulfilment following the decisive defeat of evil on the cross – not least the defeat of the evil that human empire characteristically does! Already we begin to sense two things: that if there is any 'correspondence' theory of truth implicit here (one of the normal analyses of 'truth' is that it is the 'correspondence' between a statement and something in 'the way things are'), it is a correspondence not only to the way the creation *is*, but to the way *it is intended to be* and in Jesus is now becoming. For genuine 'truth' to correspond simply to the way the world is would be to collude with the distortion of the present creation brought about by evil; that, John implies, is what happens when humans, without grace to open their eyes and hearts, attempt to tell the truth, only to see it collapse into fantasies of power. Within that context, Jesus' attempt to tell the truth – the truth of God's new creation, of the rejection of evil at every level and the reaffirmation of the created order – is bound to lead directly to conflict, as we find in John 8.

The relevant passage opens with Jesus' challenge to the Jerusalemite hearers, who are described to begin with as those who had believed in him: 'If you continue in my word, you will truly be my disciples; and you will know the truth, and the truth will set you free.'[10] This precipitates a bizarre dialogue, opening with the denial by his hearers that they have ever been enslaved to anyone. As John's readers know, this constitutes the erasure of some of the most seminal moments in their own history, the Exodus itself and then the Babylonian exile, which for many second-Temple Jews was still continuing (in a theological sense[11]). This denial of both past and present enslavement means that they cannot then hear the truth which Jesus is speaking, because this truth is the truth of their past story, their present reality and their divinely promised future, all of which depend on the truth which Jesus *is* as well as the truth he is telling. In other words, it is the truth that, in Jesus, God's creative Word has come to deal with evil and slavery and bring about the new creation.

The result is a fresh analysis of the threat that these same Judaeans have posed to Jesus because of their rejection of his message. 'Now you seek to kill me,' declares Jesus, 'someone who has told you the truth I heard from God.' By contrast, the evil power that has spread its corruption throughout the world, and even within God's chosen people, is a liar and the father of lies, and is thus the archetypal murderer. Murder is one of the founding lies of the corrupt world, the attempt to say in action that creation (or the part of creation represented by this human being before me) is a bad thing and that the only solution is to kill it. But, Jesus goes on, 'because I am telling you the truth, you don't believe me' (even though they know his life is blameless). The larger context of the chapter as a whole – arguably the strangest and darkest in John – indicates what is at stake: a new reality is being brought to birth within the cosmos, and within Israel, a reality which relativizes all other realities. And in order to perceive this new reality it is necessary to trust Jesus, since he is the creative Word through whom, as a fresh gift of grace, it is coming about. The chapter therefore leads naturally into chapter 9, where the healing of the man born blind becomes the occasion for the equally challenging teaching about whether people can see what God is doing, or whether they will remain blind, and culpably so.

This picture of Jesus as the one who speaks the unexpected, unpalatable and even unbelievable truth is thus part of the direct outworking of the prologue, rooted as it is in the creation story. The 'truth' is not a claim to power; nor is it a hidden reality either about 'the way the world is' or about 'the deep interiority' of Jesus' listeners. It is the truth about *what God is doing* to rescue creation from the evil which has infected it and to bring about new creation as the true fulfilment of the creative purpose itself. We should not be surprised, then, at the striking statement in John 14.6, famously unbelievable within both modernity and postmodernity: 'I am the way, and the truth and the life. No one comes to the father except through me.' Sadly, that saying has often been used as a badge of Christian triumphalism, and has equally been spurned for the same reasons. But it is deeply consistent with the creational and new-creational notion of truth we have begun to observe. John 14 is the making explicit of the themes that are compact and implicit within the prologue itself: 'No one has ever seen God, but the only-begotten God who is in the bosom of the father has made him known' (1.18). Thus, 'the one who has seen me has seen the father' (14.9). If it is true that Jesus is the one through whom creation is to be healed and renewed – and that is the underlying claim that both modernity and postmodernity find insulting, shocking, distasteful and discreditable – then of course he is the 'truth', and of course he reveals the father.

Any suggestion that this truth is itself a claim to power, in any sense that Nietzsche, Foucault or anyone else might object to, is massively deconstructed by the great scene with which we began, where Jesus speaks the truth to the power of Caesar's agent, knowing perfectly well that it will lead to his own horrible and shameful death. The narrative of the trial before Pilate leads from the claim to kingship and kingdom to the claim about truth, to Pilate's cynical question, the substitution of Jesus and Barabbas, the famous *Ecce Homo*, the debate about authority, and to the final, devastating self-incrimination of the Jewish leaders – 'We have no king but Caesar'. And all this is the necessary contextualizing of the apparently ridiculous, almost hubristic claim of John's incarnate Word to be the truth, to speak the truth, to reveal and bear witness to the truth. Precisely because modernity is in love with empire, and because postmodernity ends up paradoxically colluding with it, neither of these movements, which have so conditioned the way we see and hear things, can bear to entertain the possibility that the evil which has infected the world goes deeper, down to the very heart of our posturing and pretended power, and that the only solution is the deeply humbling one of the crucifixion of the Word made flesh as the ultimate witness to the ultimate truth. Thus Jesus goes to his death in order to complete the work of dealing with the evil within the existing creation and thereby opening the possibility for the new creation to be born: *tetelestai* in 19.30 echoes the 'finished' of Genesis 2.2.

And with that is revealed the full meaning of the claim which has resonated throughout the gospel, the claim that confronts the Nietzschean deconstruction of the truth-claim into a power-claim: this is, after all, a story of sheer, grace-inspired *love*. 'God so loved the world that he gave his only son'; 'This is why the father loves me, because I lay down my life, that I may receive it again'; 'Having loved his own who were in the world, Jesus loved them to the end'; 'As the father has loved me, so have I loved you; abide in my love'; 'Greater love has no one than this, to lay down one's life for one's friends; you are my friends if you do what I command you'; 'I made known to them your name, so that the love with which you loved me may be in them, and I in them.'[12] And this, as I shall now try to argue, is the ultimate answer to the postmodern challenge, not as a way back to modernist arrogance but as a way through and on to wisdom. Modernity reduced love to romantic sentimentalism; postmodernity reduced it to money, sex and power. Jesus spoke of it, and acted it out, as the ultimate meaning of truth itself, and as the ultimate mode of knowing necessary to apprehend and speak that truth.

All this comes to spectacular (though dense and puzzling) expression in the promise of the Spirit of Truth. This is a major leitmotif in the Johannine Farewell Discourses, occurring three times in a steady crescendo. We take each passage in turn.

First, in John 14.15–17: 'If you love me,' declares Jesus, 'you will keep my commands. And I will ask the father, and he will give you another helper, to be with you for ever. This other helper is the spirit of truth. The world can't receive him, because it doesn't see him or know him. But you know him, because he lives with you, and will be in you.'

Three striking things stand out here for our purposes. First, the spirit is as it were the replacement, within the calling of the disciples, of Jesus himself. Jesus is leaving, but the spirit will effectively do for the disciples what Jesus had been doing, only more so: in particular, here, manifesting the truth, as a good advocate must. But the spirit will cut clean across the way the world presently is. The disciples will receive this spirit as they do what Jesus commanded them, which, as we know from the previous chapter, is summed up in the command to love one another and thereby reveal themselves to the world as Jesus' followers. But 'the world' – the world as in the Prologue and so frequently elsewhere, that is, the world which remains in rebellion against its creator and lord – will not receive this spirit; just as it has failed to recognize Jesus, so it will fail to recognize the spirit. In other words, it will fail to acknowledge that those who are indwelt and informed by this spirit are indeed speaking and living the truth. This is no easy promise of a 'new spiritual experience', giving its privileged possessors a fresh type of spiritual excitement. It is an enabling commission for those who will follow Jesus into the world to bear an always risky witness to the truth.

Second, in John 15.26–27: 'When the helper comes – the one I shall send you from the father, the spirit of truth who comes from the father – he will give evidence about me. And you will give evidence as well, because you have been with me from the start.'

This promise of the 'helper' or 'advocate' is sandwiched between two stark and explicit longer paragraphs about the world's hatred of Jesus, and even of the father, and (in prospect at least) of the disciples also. 'The world' here turns out to be not least 'the world as it has become instantiated within the Jewish people', focused on the leaders who will shortly declare that they have no king but Caesar, and will end up putting Jesus' followers out of the synagogues. The 'spirit of truth' in this passage is therefore, again, not one who merely guarantees Jesus' followers a new tranquillity, an ease of soul or freedom from worry. Indeed, it is almost as though the coming of the spirit will intensify the opposition between Jesus' followers and 'the world'. The spirit, it seems, is given to enable the disciples to continue to bear witness in the teeth of incomprehension, opposition and persecution.

This is the context for the third and most remarkable of the promises concerning the spirit of truth: John 16.8–15. This is a dense and difficult passage and we must take it slowly.

> 'When [the spirit] comes,' said Jesus, 'he will prove the world to be in the wrong on three counts: sin, justice, and judgment. In relation to sin – because they don't believe in me. In relation to justice – because I'm going to the father, and you won't see me any more. In relation to judgment – because the ruler of this world is judged.
>
> 'There are many things I still have to say to you,' Jesus continued, 'but you're not yet strong enough to take them. When the spirit of truth comes, though, he will guide you in all the truth. He won't speak on his own account, you see, but he will speak whatever he hears. He will announce to you what's to come. He will glorify me, because he will take what belongs to me and will announce it to you. Everything that the father has is mine. That's why I said that he would take what is mine and announce it to you.'

The promise that the spirit will lead Jesus' followers into all truth is commonly invoked in the church to justify innovations of various kinds, though in and of itself it can scarcely bear the weight that is routinely placed upon it.[13] Rather, it speaks almost in riddles about the work of the spirit, in terms of the divine law court within which the spirit is to act as advocate. The spirit will make the winning case against 'the world', that is, especially those who have opposed Jesus. And this case will be made in respect of three particulars: sin, 'vindication' or (in the normal though potentially misleading translation) 'righteousness', and judgment. In each case, a brief explanation is given, though these are, to us, almost as dense and puzzling as the basic statements themselves.

Note, to begin with, that the nrsv translation, which says that the spirit 'will prove the world wrong about' sin, righteousness and judgment, is misleading. The spirit will not merely show that the world has *held incorrect opinions* on these subjects; rather, the spirit will demonstrate, as in a law court, that the world is *in the wrong*, culpable, in relation to them. The point of this judgment, this verdict for which the advocate will successfully press, is to pronounce God's judgment on 'the world', much as in Daniel 7 the heavenly court finds in favour of the people of the saints of the Most High and against the monsters from the sea. And the purpose of this judgment is not for the sake of punishment, but for the sake of putting to rights that which is wrong – in other words, for naming and dealing with the evil that has infected the world, and so to bring about God's new, renewed creation. Thus the spirit will argue for truth within a dangerous and contested world, a world that has bought heavily into lies and lived by them, missing the mark in terms of the original creation and in terms of the new one. And the spirit will do this, fully appropriately in terms of John's Christology, in relation to Jesus himself.

Thus the world is 'in the wrong' in relation to sin, because it has not believed in Jesus; that is, the symptom and measure of the world's 'missing the mark' is that it has failed to recognize Jesus as the true revelation of the father, the world's creator. Second, the spirit will prove the world guilty in relation to 'righteousness', which I take in the sense of 'vindication': Jesus is to be vindicated, exalted to the father, and the spirit will press the point home, that 'the world' – which has assumed he was in the wrong, and to be got rid of – will stand ashamed. Third, the spirit will prove the world guilty in relation to judgment, because the creator God is putting the creation to rights, and is finding 'the ruler of this world' guilty and passing sentence on him. This 'ruler' has already been mentioned in 12.31 and 14.30. The phrase clearly refers at one level to Caesar and his officers, and at another to the dark power who stands behind them, the quasi-personal force of evil that has infected and corrupted the good creation and whose work can be seen not least in the abuse of power characteristic of the empire, and ultimately (as in chapter 8) in the desire to kill. From chapter 12 onwards, the eye is drawn forwards once more to the confrontation between Jesus and Pilate, with all its heavy-laden language about kingdom, power and truth, and to its conclusion in Jesus' deeply paradoxical victory. By that victory, through the crucifixion in which it will appear that the ruler of the world is casting him out and condemning him, Jesus will in fact pass judgment on the ruler himself, and cast him out.

In terms of the triple theme of this book, this solemn promise of judgment has a triple effect. First, it is the other side of the coin of the doctrine of creation. The world is not for ever to be left in darkness while the liberated soul flies free; God will put the world to rights, liberating it not from spatio-temporal materiality but from the wickedness of the powers who at present rule it. Second, therefore, this judgment is God's victory over the principalities and powers who abuse their God-given authority in order to suppress the truth, the truth about creation and human beings, in order to further their own power. Third, in relation to the specific theme of the present chapter, this judgment is the ultimate work of the spirit of truth, calling the world and its power structures to account and so naming and dealing with the problem to which postmodernity has drawn attention but for which it has no solution.

Now at last we discover that, in Johannine terms at least, these three themes are very closely conjoined. The rule of the empire has enticed some to seek to flee the world altogether, and others to shrug their shoulders and give up on the notion of truth altogether. But the biblical narrative of creation and new creation (the latter being effected through the passing of judgment on evil within the world, and through the work of the spirit of truth) announces good news from the one true

83

God and declares that the world is indeed being put to rights. It announces that Jesus is taking his place as its rightful lord, its healer, its steward, the first-fruits of the new creation.

But how will the spirit of truth do all this? Clearly, through the witness of the church. And let me say, as clearly as possible, that when I say 'the church' here I do not mean 'the Church of England and others like it', or any other category limited in space and time. I mean the whole great company of those who name the name of Jesus, whether like Martin Luther King and Desmond Tutu they speak the truth to power from a position of social and cultural weakness, or whether like the tens of thousands marching to protest against global debt they come from ordinary middle- or working-class homes and from fifty different Christian denominations, or whether they are the little groups in the second and third century who refused to conform to the demands of the empire and died, often horribly, for their witness. Where Christian people care enough, they will find a way to make their voice heard both against the wickedness inflicted by some rulers and against the secularism that would ban us from the table altogether. The church – in this full and complete and much-wider-than-local sense – will not sit back passively and watch from the sidelines as the spirit passes sentence on the world by some other means. It will be the church's task to articulate the truth to which the spirit bears witness, which is why Jesus warns his followers that they will incur the same hostility as he has done, and with the same likely result. Jesus' disciples are called, in the power of the spirit, not indeed to announce the kind of 'judgment' envisaged by the dualist who wants to blow the world to smithereens so that he or she can end up sitting on a cloud playing a harp, but rather to announce that 'judgment' which is God's putting-to-rights of all that is wrong in the world. This is God's victory over the powerful evil that has infected the world, and is therefore not the abolition of the cosmos but its remaking. In other words, as we saw in Chapter 1, the church is called to bear witness to Jesus' death and resurrection and to the meaning which John, in company with the other New Testament writers, gives to those cataclysmic events. When the spirit comes, we note once more, this gift of God is not given in order to enable the church simply to enjoy new spiritual experiences. The spirit comes to equip the church for the hard and costly task of bearing witness to the overthrow of the world's powers, to the exaltation of Jesus as Lord in their place, and to the renewal of creation itself.

In doing so, the church is called to know, to speak and to do the truth. How can we envisage this task, granted the massive hermeneutic of suspicion which soaks in to us today through every pore? How can we invoke the spirit of truth in a world of postmodernity, whose spokespersons are all around us, not least within the church itself?

Knowing, speaking and doing the truth

For a start, we note certain principles. In offering a critique of postmodernity I am certainly not suggesting that we should return from postmodernity to the cheerful but shallow certainties of modernity, whether secular modernity or Christian modernity. The world is far more complex than modernity ever allowed, and if there is such a thing as truth it will be discerned and spoken in far more subtle and interesting ways than modernity ever imagined.

Furthermore, 'knowing the truth' is, it seems, a *public* activity. It is not a matter of the secret, hidden knowledge of the gnostic. Nor is it a matter of mere assertion within private groups. It is rather a matter of speech and action which offers itself within and to the world of creation and new creation, offers itself in *testimony* before the watching and evaluating world.

Knowing, speaking and doing the truth must always therefore, however paradoxical, be a *humble* affair. The church knows its own witness to be frail and partial and in need of constant correction and guidance, so that even when it is speaking and acting it reminds itself that there is yet more to be learnt. The church, if it is to be truly itself, can never risk aping the powers and authorities which, though called to bring God's order into the otherwise chaotic world, decide to abuse that calling and so themselves contribute to the chaos. Rather, the church must constantly invoke the spirit, must speak of Jesus and his death and resurrection, and must bear witness to the goodness of creation, the defeat of evil, and the launching and final promise of new creation.

But those themes, which as will be clear to the observant reader are my subtext throughout this book, are not merely the things about which the church must speak, and in harmony with which the church must act. They themselves, rooted in the work of Jesus and the spirit, form the ontological and epistemological groundwork for a reappraised, perhaps even a repristinated, view of what truth is, and what it means to know it, to speak it and to do it.

Truth, it appears, is not simply a matter of stating the way things are within the world. The world, though itself good, is out of joint. To attempt to describe the world of creation by itself is to fail to pay attention to the radical evil that has infected it. Paradoxically, a mere description of how things are in the present time will be a lie, a collusion with the distortion of truth brought about by the corruption and enslavement of the world and particularly of humans – humans, who should have been the great truth-tellers, the animal-namers (as in Genesis 2), but who worshipped and served the creation rather than the Creator. Simply to attempt a mere 'correspondence' kind of truth would thus be to run the inevitable risk that the evil which is distorting the world will distort also the motives and meanings of those who attempt, naively, to describe it. Truth must therefore belong *in the interplay between creation, judgment and new creation*. The *possibility* of truth is rooted in the goodness of creation, but the *finding* and *speaking* of truth is rooted in God's judgment on the corruption of that creation and his accomplishment of its rescue and renewal. God's word of judgment and renewal opens the possibility of a fresh word which is not a lie, not a collusion with corruption.

If this is so, then the finding of truth in the sense of 'knowing' must lie within the human vocation to be God's image-bearers within creation, entrusted with the responsibility of taking forward God's purposes for that world; and then within the precarious but spirit-sustained vocation to be *renewed* image-bearers, people in whose knowing God can 'know' the new world into being. But this 'knowing' can never be reduced to the terms of the shallow objectivity beloved within modernism. Nor, for that matter, can it be reduced to the collapsing subjectivity insisted on within postmodernity. In order to know the truth, as becomes increasingly clear throughout John's gospel, the church is called to do so through *love*. Love, as we observed before, cannot be reduced to the romantic periphery of epistemology, as in modernism, or the mere projection of desire, as in postmodernity. Love, when it is the love of which the Johannine Jesus speaks so frequently, is the mode of knowing in which the object of love is fully affirmed, cherished and valued, but in which simultaneously the knower is fully involved as a delighted, appreciative, celebratory participant. Love thus transcends the subjective/objective divide, affirming both epistemological poles in a way Western epistemologies have so often failed to do. And, as Wittgenstein memorably remarked, 'it is *love* that believes the resurrection': because it is love that, looking at creation in its corrupt and decaying state, dares to speak the word of judgment upon that corruption and the word of new life that heals and renews. And it dares to do this because it responds in faith to God as creator and to Jesus as Lord, and believes in the renewing power of the spirit to enable it to know the truth which, if reduced beyond this triple story of creation, judgment and new creation, is actually falsified.

This is the point where genuine art is a form of true knowing, a response to the very beauty of God. Only when we redefine both beauty and truth within a Trinitarian theology of judgment and new creation can we affirm Keats' dictum that 'beauty is truth, truth beauty'. Without that framework, the proposal collapses either into sentiment or into an over-intellectual aesthetic.

From knowing, then, to speaking. As Paul says, we are to speak the truth in love. This is not simply to be taken as a reminder that, when we tell one another the truth, we should do so lovingly. It means, rather, that the truth which we are called on to speak, as followers of Jesus, is a truth which grows out of that which is known only by love, and which can therefore only be spoken out of that same love. Jesus' followers are called to be those through whom words of judgment can be spoken over the corruption of evil, and words of life can be spoken to bring new creation to birth. In line with the human vocation to name the animals in Genesis 2, the followers of Jesus are called, in the power of the spirit, to use human words to speak the complex but rich truth about God and the world – not, once more, as esoteric, hidden knowledge, available only to the elite in private, but as dangerous and contested public truth which calls the rulers to account and speaks powerfully of new creation – indeed, uses speech to *bring about* new creation. Our project of truth-telling, rooted in the epistemology of love, cannot be merely a matter of 'objective' description of the way things are, but must be part of God's work of calling the corrupted world to account and pointing on towards new creation. Speech like this is therefore *prophetic*, listening for God's word of judgment and grace and then speaking it to the world the way it is, sharing, as prophetic speech always does, in the work of bringing about that which it announces. Not to speak thus, or to speak otherwise than thus, will be to lie, not so much in failing to describe what is there before the senses, but in failing to speak truly, with genuine human wisdom, about the totality of what is there from, if we dare say so, God's point of view.

This is where, once more, we can understand something of the true *political* speech of the church (and once again this is not 'the church' as 'the established church' but 'the church' as 'the whole people of God in Christ, often precisely when they are marginalized and suffering'). We must never forget that when Pilate asked Jesus if he was a king, Jesus offered a more exact description: 'call me king if you must, but the sovereignty I exercise is that of bearing witness to the truth.'[14] Reading John 16 in the light of that later claim indicates, alarmingly, that the truth-speaking vocation which we have been exploring is a *royal* vocation, a sharing of Jesus' own Messianic vocation such as can only be explained – but then is fully explained – in terms of the breathing of the spirit upon the disciples after the resurrection, giving them authority to forgive and retain sins.[15] And this indicates once more that the mission to which the disciples are sent is not a 'spiritual' mission only, but (in today's language at least) a political one. Today's polarized (and trivialized) political discourse has tended to oscillate between those who want merely to describe things as they are – the first word, indeed, which needs to be spoken – and those who want merely to call down judgment on the way things are – the second word which needs to be spoken. But followers of Jesus can never remain content with either the one (as though there were not such a thing as radical evil) or the other (as though we were after all to revert to dualism). We need both, the powerful affirmation ('Look! This is how things are!') and the vital critique ('Look! All is not well!'). But we need, also, the third word which speaks prophetically and truly of new creation, God's fresh lifegiving word after the critique has been heard, after the last echoes of deconstruction have been hushed in the darkness of the tomb. It is on the first day of the new week that Mary Magdalene goes to the tomb and speaks the new, true word about Jesus' resurrection; and it is on the evening of that day that Jesus breathes on the disciples and, equipping them with the spirit, with all the echoes of the earlier passages at which we have looked, commissions them to be for the world what he had been for Israel: 'As the Father sent me, so I send you.' And the disciples are thus sent out to speak words of truth into the world that is still unready for them, words of judgment and new creation, truth that is not merely descriptive but also evaluative and creative, truth that some will speak in words and others in music and others still in silent but powerful deeds of love.

We need to remember that the New Testament speaks of truth not simply as something to know and something to speak but as something to *do*. Those who follow Jesus are called to be people through whom the corruptions of the world can be overcome, and signs of the new creation brought to birth. There is much one could say about this, but not here. Suffice it to note with delight that many branches of today's church are increasingly realizing this vocation and are finding, in addition, that working together at doing the truth in practical ways in the wider community is an excellent way of learning theological truth side by side and so growing together at every level.

Where has all this taken us in terms of the postmodern turn and its challenge to the very notion of truth, let alone of a spirit of truth? We have arrived at a Trinitarian understanding of the gospel for our culture, which generates a different set of answers to the four questions to which modernity and postmodernity gave their key answers. We have glimpsed a vision of a God who is neither an absentee landlord nor merely the pantheistic life or soul of the world, but is the transcendent creator and who, incarnate in Jesus of Nazareth, has dealt the decisive blow to the corruption that has defaced the good creation and is already at work to remake it, starting with Jesus' resurrection. As for the world itself, it is good, and knowable as such, in virtue of its good creation, but shot through now with a corruption which has made knowledge of the world complex – the epistemological equivalent, perhaps, of the ground bringing forth thorns and thistles after the Fall. But the world, though to be judged in its corrupt state, is also to be remade, so that eventually, as Paul and John and other early Christians insisted, heaven and earth shall be one. And in this vision not only truth but also beauty are to be understood and celebrated. As for the 'self', the hero of modernity and the empty raincoat in postmodernity, it is remade – not rediscovered, as in Gnosticism, but given new life, new birth, through the sheer grace and power of the creator's love. And the story in which all this is encapsulated is not a progress-story, as though new creation were simply able to grow quietly out of the old, as though there were no corruption and evil to be faced and beaten at tremendous cost, but rather the story of judgment and mercy, of the creator's utter rejection of evil and his powerful lifegiving energy, of cross and resurrection.

To believe this story, let alone to live by it, will mean to work it out in a spirituality not of Gnosticism, nor yet of pantheism, but of the celebration of creation, judgment and new creation in Jesus Christ and in the power of the spirit. To do this will mean, in turn, learning to speak the truth to power, a task more urgent than ever in our day. And when the powers of the world use the postmodern rhetoric to sneer at our attempts to speak that truth, we must take courage, invoke the spirit, and become people through whom the Advocate can do the necessary work of convicting the world in respect of sin, righteousness and judgment; people who, with the breath of Jesus in our nostrils, can be for the world what he was for Israel. The triple contemporary challenge of *gnosis*, empire and postmodernity, which sustain and support one another in so many ways in today's world, can and must be met by the good news of God the creator, of Jesus the Lord, of the spirit of truth. That is the way the church must travel if we are to find our way through postmodernity and out the other side, through the horrible ambiguities of empire and on towards a more mature role in the world, and through the problems of the present creation to discover and anticipate the promised new creation. The Christian gospel has, no doubt, much more than this to say to our culture, but not, I think, any less. There is work to be done in this coming generation, and readers of this book may be some of the people who ought to be doing it.

Conclusion

So, to conclude, I address in particular those who want to take the Christian gospel seriously and navigate their way through the cultural and social minefield I have been describing. What does the Christian gospel say, and equally important what does it do, within the confusing world we live in?

The main theme of the Christian gospel is of course love – as the recently retired Pope Benedict insisted from the start of his first encyclical. But we have so routinely sentimentalized that truth (which Benedict didn't, by the way) that we have then failed to realize how the love of which the gospel speaks confronts rival worldviews. And since Christian life and work are all about the multiple overflowings and outworkings of God's love, it is vital that we reflect on this as we commit ourselves to serving Jesus Christ in his world.

Because it *is* his world, as the New Testament insists, building foursquare on the Old Testament and confronting as it does so all Gnosticisms ancient and modern. *Gnosis*, says St Paul, puffs you up; but love builds you up. What matters, he says, is not your *gnosis*, your knowledge of this or that, but the fact that the one creator God knows you. That is 1 Corinthians 8, where Paul goes on to expound Jewish-style monotheism, rethought around Jesus Christ, as the sheet-anchor of the Christian gospel and ministry. The doctrine of creation, and then the promise of new creation brought about by God's judgment and mercy, are thus the foundation of genuinely Christian, and for that matter Jewish, thought and life. God made the world out of overflowing love; one day, God will put the world finally to rights out of overflowing love in the form of justice, the justice that refuses to allow the world to be destroyed and pillaged any further. In between those two moments, grounding and validating that theology

93

and energizing the work of the gospel, stands the fact of Jesus Christ himself, the one through whom all things were made, becoming himself a creature within his own world, sharing the death that the empire inflicts on those who live and announce God's kingdom, and rising again as the launching-pad of God's new creation. This is the fresh word from God, always rooted in history but always new, which like the best navigation system will address us anew no matter where we've got ourselves to. This is precisely what the gnostic does not want to see; it is precisely what the empire does not want to hear; it is precisely what makes the postmodernist reach for Derrida with one hand and Valium with the other.

All Christian work derives directly from that work of Jesus Christ. All genuinely Christian teaching must therefore confront Gnosticism of whatever sort and show it up for what it is, refuting its critiques not by political suppression but by the powerful message of new creation, lived out in spirit-led communities where the alienation which drives people into Gnosticism is dealt with not by escapism but, once more, by love. Communities like that can never be self-serving or inward-looking, but will in their very nature be working to put into practice that new creation which Jesus began, implementing his achievement and thereby anticipating the day when God will put all things to rights. Christian work for justice in the present flows directly, as again Benedict saw in his various encyclicals, from the imperative of Christian love. One of the main arguments against Gnosticism is that it cuts the nerve of that work, of that ministry.

But if the Christian gospel rules out Gnosticism it must also confront the empire with which Gnosticism colludes. Jesus is Lord, declares Paul, in passages which make it clear that he means, 'and so Caesar is not'. The resurrection of Jesus establishes him as Israel's Messiah and the world's true king, which is naturally why not only Gnosticism but also the empire have had to deny it (in our day the empire has made good use of the supposedly neutral, but in fact heavily loaded, historiography of the Enlightenment). But, as in Colossians, once the powers have been defeated and led as bedraggled captives in Jesus' triumphal procession, they are not abolished but reconciled. The task of the church is not to oppose on principle all those in authority, but to hold up before the authorities a measured and nuanced critique based on the justice we see in the gospel of Jesus and in God's plan to sum up all things in heaven and on earth in him.

At this point we must note that a genuinely Christian political theology must affirm the goodness of rulers and authorities, of legislators and law enforcers, precisely because this world is God's world and because God will put it to rights at the last. God does not want the world, in the meantime, to collapse into chaos and anarchy. The task of rulers and authorities is thus to bring a measure of anticipated putting-to-rights to God's world, a measure of inaugurated eschatology. To that end the church must encourage the authorities to go to their God-given task, while cheerfully but relentlessly critiquing them when they abuse this vocation for their own ends. This must work at local, national and global levels. I thank God for the way this is happening in, for instance, the global campaigns for remission of international debt and for serious and urgent action to combat climate change, in both of which campaigns Christians have rightly been prominent.

All this generates a particular and important reflection, developing further something I said earlier. The early Christians, like their Jewish contemporaries, were not particularly concerned with how the rulers got to be rulers. They were very concerned with what they did *as* rulers. I suspect that we in the West have got this the wrong way round, with our implicit belief that as long as people vote from time to time what their elected representatives then do must somehow be validated. And this, in turn, has implied that the church has no more role to play. I believe we must find the way to the opposite conclusion. The church in our day, led by the spirit and seeking fresh wisdom in prayer and study of scripture, must discover the way, against howls of protest no doubt, to reinstate the role of religion, of faith, within the public square, refusing to accept the sneering instruction to go back into private life where we belong. It is the failure of the Western world to deal with the public meaning of faith that created the vacuum into which September 11 burst with such spectacular horror. Today's church, with all the varied ministries it contains, must give itself to the task not only of speaking the truth to power (as Jesus did to Pontius Pilate), but also *living* the truth under the nose of power, as Paul did when he arrived in Rome in Acts 28. This is how not only we, but perhaps also our culture, may indeed hear a fresh word from God in these troubled times.

September 11, 2001 was a kind of ultimate postmodern moment, the clash of mutually destructive grand narratives. Since then we have seen a confused and dangerous aftermath, as people on all sides scramble for what's left of the international moral high ground, only to discover that they have forgotten how to do moral discourse at all in the morass of Gnosticism, imperialism and postmodernity itself, let alone how to think wisely about the place of religion in public life without collapsing into fundamentalism or retreating into secularism.

Here again we need to reappropriate the meaning of love, love as action on the one hand and love as epistemology on the other. We don't just 'know' things with an objectivity outside ourselves, or with a subjectivity that then collapses into a private world. True knowledge is a mode of love, of that generosity which listens and waits and pays attention to the object of love in order to enter into a living and appropriate relation with that other. That remains as urgent a task in the political as it does in the personal sphere. Love leads us out of our ant-like vicious circles and forwards under the fresh direction of the God who creates, who judges, who speaks.

Within postmodernity love appears as a mirage, since it becomes deconstructed into power, sex and money. What the Christian gospel offers, and what Christian movements must urgently offer in their formation of communities of faith, hope, prayer and witness, is a love which cannot be deconstructed, a love which manifestly is seeking its neighbour's good rather than its own, a love which goes out into the public square not in order to gain power, prestige or money but in order to incarnate that love of God which is expressed precisely in God's putting of all things to rights, God's righteousness, God's justice. That work of overflowing love – the work of all Christian ministry at whatever level and in whatever form – is the ultimate and best answer to Gnosticism, to imperialism, and to postmodernity itself. The gospel of Jesus Christ thus addresses, through the varied ministries of the church, not simply the individual needs of individual human beings, but the large issues in which so many in today's world are getting bogged down and becoming helpless and hopeless.

And yet, wonderfully, the individual needs are not thereby sidestepped, but are fully taken into account. The deepest personal answer to Gnosticism is that self-knowledge which comes as a fresh gift: 'the Son of God loved me', said St Paul, 'and gave himself for me.'[1] The deepest personal answer to living under empire is to worship Jesus as Lord from the bottom of your heart, and to determine to give him your allegiance in the public world as well as the private. And, when faced with postmodernity's version of the doctrine of original sin, the Christian gospel offers, and offers through all the spirit-driven ministries of the church, the living and embodied doctrine of redemption: the true story of the world and of ourselves within it, which cannot be deconstructed because it is a love-story; the true knowledge of the world and of ourselves and of God, not as objective truth over against ourselves nor as subjective truth merely but as truth known in and through love; and the true identity of being called in the spirit to be children of God. All this shows up today's emphasis on 'tolerance' for what it is. 'Tolerance', today's buzz-word, is merely a thin parody of love; I can tolerate you standing on the other side of the road, without needing to engage with you at all. Love is a harder, higher and ultimately redemptive calling, the fresh voice of the God who speaks to lead us out of our aimless cultural wanderings.

It is genuine Christ-shaped love, therefore, embodied in our varied ministries and callings and spoken as a fresh word into our culture, that provides the ultimate answer to the follies and the false trails of our day. The Christian gospel, because it is all about embodied love, is easily robust and many-sided enough to take on tomorrow's world and make it a place where good news goes out and flourishes, good news for the poor and the hungry, the homeless and the drug addicts, the rich and the lonely, the religious and the sceptical. My hope and prayer is that this book will help stir up the vocations of many readers to engage with God's world, and with our confusing culture, to live the gospel as well as to preach it, to make it happen on earth as in heaven.

Notes

1 God the creator in a world of neo-Gnosticism

1 Dan Brown, *The Da Vinci Code* (London: Corgi, 2004).

2 Michael A. Williams, *Rethinking Gnosticism: An Argument for Dismantling a Dubious Category* (Princeton: Princeton University Press, 1996); Karen L. King, *What is Gnosticism?* (Cambridge, MA: Harvard University Press, 2003).

3 Perhaps the scholarly oscillation between the two has more to do with types of personality and preferred method – and perhaps with an implicit preference between Plato and Aristotle – than with any ultimate veracity.

4 E.g. James M. Robinson; Marvin Meyer; Bart Ehrman. My sense is that Karen King protests too much against definitions produced from Irenaeus and Tertullian; the Nag Hammadi and other texts – not least the newly published *The Gospel of Judas* – give strong indications of these central features.

5 Philip J. Lee, *Against the Protestant Gnostics* (New York: Oxford University Press, 1993); C. O'Regan, *Gnostic Return in Modernity* (Albany, NY: State University Press of New York, 2001); also, much criticized but still important, Harold Bloom (see below).

6 Similar trends within Judaism are fascinatingly tracked by Jon D. Levenson in his recent monograph, *Resurrection and the Restoration of Israel: The Ultimate Victory of the God of Life* (New Haven: Yale University Press, 2006).

7 A. N. Wilson, *God's Funeral* (London: Abacus, 2000).

8 See Tom Wolfe, *The Bonfire of the Vanities* (New York: Farrar, Straus & Giroux, 1987).

9 Richard Dawkins, *The God Delusion* (London: Bantam Press, 2006), p. 31. Dawkins does allow that 'Gentle Jesus' owes more to Victorian piety than to Jesus himself.

10 See Ch. 2.

11 See Tom Wright, *Judas and the Gospel of Jesus* (London: SPCK, 2006).

12 See especially the first three volumes of N. T. Wright, Christian Origins and the Question of God: *The New Testament and the*

People of God (London: SPCK, 1992); *Jesus and the Victory of God* (London: SPCK, 1996); *The Resurrection of the Son of God* (London: SPCK, 2003), and not least the fourth one, *Paul and the Faithfulness of God* (London: SPCK, forthcoming).

13 Of course, churches that go this route often find themselves opposing 'mainline' or 'orthodox' Christian teaching; but that is simply the stock-in-trade of late modernity and, unlike the dangerous witness of the second-century churches it requires little courage or theological acumen.

14 I am well aware that some fundamentalist groups, not least within African-American traditional Christianity, have combined an effectively pre-modern theology and hermeneutic with a decidedly this-worldly and even liberationist ethic. There are more ironies and variations here than it is possible to map in the present book.

15 It would be interesting to explore the genealogy of this comparative lack. It might be found to have something to do with the deep suspicion of natural theology or indeed any positive evaluation of the created order, under Barthian influence on the one hand or that of Bultmann's neo-Kantian Lutheranism on the other. In the latter case, it was even seriously proposed that some of the key texts, such as John 1 or Colossians 1, started life as gnostic poems and were then lightly Christianized – a theory which I regard as desperate to the point of absurdity. Then, with the turn to Jewish history-of-religions matrices for early Christianity in the second half of the last century, attention was focused not so much on creation – though there is plenty about it in the relevant texts – but on such matters as the 'third quest' for Jesus and the 'new perspective' on Paul, in both of which in my judgment creation plays a vital role but one which remains less explored. And despite the (to me) obvious advantages of a deeply creational reading of the Old Testament for the various liberationist readings of the New Testament, once again the theme has not been prominent – perhaps not least because of the deep suspicion in some areas for the Hebrew scriptures, particularly Genesis, as a source for appropriate and available Christian theology. There are of

course exceptions, among which is the notable recent monograph of T. R. Jackson, *New Creation in Paul's Letters* (Tübingen: Mohr Siebeck, 2010). Jackson notes others who have contributed on this theme.

16 These are themselves prophecies of redemption, return from exile, and ultimately new creation.

17 Cf. John 3.16. 'Eternal life' in that verse, though regularly misunderstood (not least within a semi-gnostic evangelicalism!) in terms of 'disembodied eternity', refers, as the phrase normally does in the NT, to the Jewish 'age to come'. Hence the promise that those who believe 'will not perish'.

18 E.g. John 19.15: '"We have no king," the chief priests replied, "except Caesar!"' See Ch. 2 of the present book.

19 E.g. John 8.32: 'you will know the truth, and the truth will make you free'; John 17.3: 'And by "the life of God's coming age" I mean this: that they should know you, the only true God, and Jesus the Messiah, the one you sent.'

20 John 17.15: 'I'm not asking that you should take them out of the world, but that you should keep them from the evil one' – a key distinction, between the created order on the one hand and the evil which has infected it on the other.

21 I think, for instance, of Schmithals' attempts to see Gnosticism behind every other phrase in 1 Corinthians, and Hengel's attempts to prove him wrong. See W. Schmithals, *Paul and the Gnostics* (Nashville: Abingdon, 1972); M. Hengel and A. M. Schwemer, *Paul Between Damascus and Antioch: The Unknown Years* (London: SCM Press, 1997).

22 See Wright, *The Resurrection of the Son of God*.

23 1 Cor. 8.6.

24 See especially 1 Cor. 15.20–28.

25 See N. T. Wright, *The Climax of the Covenant: Christ and the Law in Pauline Theology* (Edinburgh: T. & T. Clark, 1991), ch. 5.

26 Cf. Phil. 3.2–6. See N. T. Wright, *Colossians and Philemon* (Leicester: Inter-Varsity Press, 1987), followed in this by J. D. G. Dunn, *The Epistles to the Colossians and to Philemon*, NIGTC (Grand Rapids: Eerdmans, 1996) and Michael Bird, *Colossians and Philemon*, New Covenant Commentaries (Eugene, OR: Cascade,

2009); see also M. D. Hooker, 'Were There False Teachers in Colosse?', in B. Lindars and S. S. Smalley (eds), *Christ and Spirit in the New Testament: Essays in Honour of Charles Francis Digby Moule* (Cambridge: Cambridge University Press, 1973), pp. 315–31.

27 So, rightly, C. C. Rowland in *Christian Origins* (London: SPCK, 1985), pp. 291–4.

28 As e.g. Pss. 96, 98, etc.

2 Jesus the Lord: the gospel and the new imperialism

1 There is a possible parallel in those Hindus who, faced with difficult political challenges, converted to Buddhism.

2 As does the proposal of some quasi-gnostic hypothetical sources behind the synoptic gospels (e.g. certain versions of the 'Q' hypothesis).

3 Cf. e.g. Niall Ferguson, *Colossus: The Rise and Fall of the American Empire* (New York: Penguin, 2004).

4 In England, this appears as the 'Whig view of history'.

5 A challenge to the normal view of early persecution has come from C. Moss, *The Myth of Persecution: How Early Christians Invented a Story of Martyrdom* (San Francisco: HarperOne, 2013). It is too soon for scholarly reaction to this book, which on the face of it appears to be another attempt at a 'new myth' of Christian origins.

6 E.g. Regina M. Schwartz, *The Curse of Cain: The Violent Legacy of Monotheism* (Chicago: University of Chicago Press, 1997).

7 John Shelton Lawrence and Robert Jewett, *The Myth of the American Superhero* (Grand Rapids: Eerdmans, 2002); Robert Jewett and John Shelton Lawrence, *Captain America and the Crusade Against Evil: The Dilemma of Zealous Nationalism* (Grand Rapids: Eerdmans, 2003).

8 See A. Sherwin-White, *Roman Society and Roman Law in the New Testament* (Oxford: Oxford University Press, 1963), pp. 24–47.

9 As introduced by the prologue's statement that 'he was in the world, and the world was made through him, and the world did not know him' (John 1.10).

10 Of whom the prologue at once goes on to say that 'he came to what was his own, and his own people did not accept him' (John 1.11).
11 John 19.11.
12 Gen. 2.2.
13 See especially N. T. Wright, *Paul: Fresh Perspectives* (London: SPCK, 2005; published in the USA as *Paul in Fresh Perspective* (Minneapolis: Augsburg Fortress) ch. 4.
14 Gal. 2.20.
15 Cf. N. T. Wright, *Paul and the Faithfulness of God*, Christian Origins and the Question of God, vol. 4 (London: SPCK, forthcoming), ch. 2.
16 Rom. 15.12.
17 The question is now of pressing interest in America: see e.g. Jim Wallis, *God's Politics* (New York: HarperCollins, 2005).
18 See N. T. Wright, *Evil and the Justice of God* (London: SPCK, 2006).

3 Spirit of Truth in a postmodern world

1 John 18.37–38.
2 John Dominic Crossan, *Jesus: A Revolutionary Biography* (New York: HarperCollins, 1994), p. 222.
3 See Bernard Williams, *Truth and Truthfulness: An Essay in Genealogy* (Princeton, NJ: Princeton University Press, 2004).
4 Nicholas Boyle, *Who Are We Now?: Christian Humanism and the Global Market from Hegel to Heaney* (Notre Dame, IN: University of Notre Dame Press, 1999).
5 Rom. 1.18–23; 2 Thess. 2.12.
6 Gal. 2.5, 14; 5.7.
7 1 Cor. 2.11–16.
8 Gal. 4.16; Eph. 4.15.
9 John 1.14, 17.
10 John 8.31–32.
11 See N. T. Wright, *Paul and the Faithfulness of God*, Christian Origins and the Question of God, vol. 4 (London: SPCK, forthcoming), ch. 2.
12 John 3.16; 10.17; 13.1; 15.9, 13; 17.26.

13 Even with help from the similar 14.26, which promises that the
spirit will teach the disciples all things, and bring to their remem-
brance what Jesus has said.

14 John 18.37.

15 John 20.23.

Conclusion

1 Gal. 2.20.

Select bibliography

Bird, M. (2009). *Colossians and Philemon*. New Covenant Commentaries. Eugene, OR: Cascade.

Boyle, Nicholas (1999). *Who Are We Now?: Christian Humanism and the Global Market from Hegel to Heaney*. Notre Dame, IN: University of Notre Dame Press.

Brown, Dan (2004). *The Da Vinci Code*. London: Corgi.

Crossan, John Dominic (1994). *Jesus: A Revolutionary Biography*. New York: HarperCollins.

Dawkins, Richard (2006). *The God Delusion*. London: Bantam Press.

Dunn, J. D. G. (1996). *The Epistles to the Colossians and to Philemon*. NIGTC. Grand Rapids: Eerdmans.

Ferguson, Niall (2004). *Colossus: The Rise and Fall of the American Empire*. New York: Penguin.

Jewett, Robert and John Shelton Lawrence (2003). *Captain America and the Crusade Against Evil: The Dilemma of Zealous Nationalism*. Grand Rapids: Eerdmans.

King, Karen L. (2003). *What is Gnosticism?*. Cambridge, MA: Harvard University Press.

Lawrence, John Shelton and Robert Jewett (2002). *The Myth of the American Superhero*. Grand Rapids: Eerdmans.

Lee, Philip J. (1993). *Against the Protestant Gnostics*. New York: Oxford University Press.

Levenson, Jon D. (2006). *Resurrection and the Restoration of Israel: The Ultimate Victory of the God of Life*. New Haven: Yale University Press.

Moss, Candida (2013). *The Myth of Persecution: How Early Christians Invented a Story of Martyrdom*. San Francisco: HarperOne.

O'Regan, C. (2001). *Gnostic Return in Modernity*. Albany, NY: State University Press of New York.

Rowland, C. C. (1985). *Christian Origins*. London: SPCK.

Sacks, Jonathan (2006). 'The prophets are our unflappable sat-nav, not the lost car in front', *The Times*, 4 February.

Schwartz, Regina M. (1997). *The Curse of Cain: The Violent Legacy of Monotheism*. Chicago: University of Chicago Press.

Wallis, Jim (2005). *God's Politics*. New York: HarperCollins.

Williams, Bernard (2004). *Truth and Truthfulness: An Essay in Genealogy*. Princeton, NJ: Princeton University Press.

Williams, Michael A. (1996). *Rethinking Gnosticism: An Argument for Dismantling a Dubious Category*. Princeton: Princeton University Press.

Wilson, A. N. (2000). *God's Funeral*. London: Abacus.

Wolfe, Tom (1987). *The Bonfire of the Vanities*. New York: Farrar, Straus & Giroux.

Wright, N. T. (1987). *Colossians and Philemon*. Tyndale New Testament Commentaries. Leicester: Inter-Varsity Press.

Wright, N. T. (1991). *The Climax of the Covenant: Christ and the Law in Pauline Theology*. Edinburgh: T. & T. Clark.

Wright, N. T. (1992). *The New Testament and the People of God*. Christian Origins and the Question of God, vol. 1. London: SPCK.

Wright, N. T. (1996). *Jesus and the Victory of God*. Christian Origins and the Question of God, vol. 2. London: SPCK.

Wright, N. T. (2005). *Paul: Fresh Perspectives*. London: SPCK. Published in the USA as *Paul in Fresh Perspective*. Minneapolis: Augsburg Fortress.

Wright, N. T. (2005). *The Resurrection of the Son of God*. Christian Origins and the Question of God, vol. 3. London: SPCK.

Wright, N. T. (2006). *Evil and the Justice of God*. London: SPCK.

Wright, N. T. (forthcoming). *Paul and the Faithfulness of God*. Christian Origins and the Question of God, vol. 4. London: SPCK.

Wright, Tom (2006). *Judas and the Gospel of Jesus*. London: SPCK.

Index of biblical references

Index of names and topics

Adorno, T. W. 66
anarchy/-ism 42, 46, 50, 52,
    61 2, 95
apocalyptic 28, 48
asceticism 8, 13
atonement 10, 52, 54–5
Augustus 51, 66

Bar-Kochba 35
Barth, Karl 100 n15
Benedict xvi 93–4
Bloom, Harold 18
Boyle, Nicholas 73
British empire 37–8
Brown, Dan 4–5, 7, 17–18
Bultmann, Rudolf 21, 100 n15

Caesar 19, 24, 36, 43, 48, 49–50,
    53, 78, 82
Christology 22, 24–7, 30, 82
Cicero 38
Constantine 17, 58
Copernicus, Nicolaus 19
creation (doctrine) 6–7, 13,
    21–9, 46, 50, 53, 55, 59–60,
    65, 83
creationism 14–15, 20
'credit crunch' 40
Crossan, Dominic 66
crucifixion 33, 49–51, 54–5, 59,
    78, 83
Cynics/-ism 66
Cyprian 44

Darwin/-ianism 13–15, 38, 42,
    72, 74

Dawkins, Richard 13–14
debt, global 40–1, 74, 84, 95
Derrida, Jacques 72, 94
Diocletian 44
dualism 14–15, 25, 33, 57, 67, 89
    of heaven/earth 6, 9, 15, 28
    of matter/spirit 23
    of reason/history 8
    of politics/theology 48

ecology 13, 30–1, 33, 42, 64, 95
emperor-cult 52
Enlightenment, the 7–8, 10–11,
    18–19, 29–31, 33, 38, 41, 54,
    58, 61–61, 68–73, 95
epistemology 86–8, 91, 96
eschatology 7, 10–11, 30, 32, 39,
    53, 95
evolution 13–14

Foucault, Michel 78
fundamentalism 18, 20, 29, 32,
    48, 71

George III 37, 57
globalization 41, 43
'gnostic gospels' 16, 18–19, 31,
    36, 47
Gnosticism 3, 4–34, 35–6, 42,
    44, 47, 56, 68–9, 91, 94, 97

heaven 7–11, 17, 20, 27, 30, 36,
    42, 48, 53, 56–7
'hermeneutic of suspicion' 67–9,
    85
Homer 19

Index of names and topics